Guidelines for Environmental Design in Schools

(Revision of Design Note 17)

Architects and Building Branch
Department for Education and Employment

London : The Stationery Office

Acknowledgements

DfEE would like to thank the following researchers:

Raf Orlowski of Arup Acoustics for **Section A**;

David Loe, Newton Watson, Edward Rowlands and Kevin Mansfield of The Bartlett School of Architecture, Building, Environmental Design and Planning, University College London for **Section B**;

Bob Venning of Ove Arup R&D for updating **Section B** and John Baker for the section on lighting for pupils with visual impairments; and

Andrew Seager, John Minikin, Richard Hobday and John Palmer of Databuild Ltd. for **Sections C, D** and **F.**

DfEE would also like to thank the members of the Local Education Authorities who provided information on various schools and the Society of Chief Electrical and Mechanical Engineers (SCEME) for their help with the project.

Particular thanks to:

Colin Grindley, Cranfield University;

Chris French, Essex County Council;

Anthony Wilson, Oscar Faber Applied Research;

Ian Hodgson, Cleveland County Council;

Alan Yates, Building Research Establishment;

Les Fothergill, Building Research Establishment;

Dave Hampton, Building Research Establishment;

Andrew Williams, Building Research Establishment;

Matthew Dickinson, Building Research Establishment;

Miles Attenborough, ECD Energy and Environment Ltd;

Duncan Templeton, BDP Acoustics Ltd;

Phil Jones, University of Wales College of Cardiff;

Derek Poole, University of Wales College of Cardiff;

Noel Deam, SCEME;

Fred Harrison, SCEME;

John Coggins, Society of Chief Architects in Local Authorities.

DfEE Project Team:

Mukund Patel, Head of Architects and Building Branch;

Chris Bissell, Principal Architect, Architects and Building Branch;

Richard Daniels, Senior Engineer, Architects and Building Branch.

ISBN 011 271013 1

Contents

Introduction (i)

Section A: Acoustics 1

Section B: Lighting 8

Section C: Heating and thermal performance 15

Section D: Ventilation 21

Section E: Hot and cold water supplies 23

Section F: Energy (carbon dioxide) rating 26
Energy (carbon dioxide) rating calculation sheet 37
Energy (carbon dioxide) rating spreadsheet formula sheet 38

Summary sheets
The School Premises Regulations summary sheet 39
Recommended constructional standards summary sheet 40

Note: *Numbered references in superscript refer to references at the end of the relevant section.*

Introduction

This publication replaces Design Note 17 *Guidelines for Environmental Design and Fuel Conservation in Educational Buildings* published in 1981.

Both existing and new school premises are required by law to comply with the minimum standards prescribed in *The Education (School Premises) Regulations* 1996. This guidance provides practical advice on meeting these standards.

New school premises which are approved by the Secretary of State are expected to comply with the constructional standards published by the Department for Education and Employment. These specify Design Note 17 as the standard for environmental design.

For ease of reference, the relevant minimum standards and the constructional standards are reproduced in boxes at the beginning of each section and are summarised on pages 39 and 40.

Although there are separate sections on the various environmental factors and on energy (carbon dioxide) ratings, the designer is encouraged to apply an holistic approach to the design. Acoustics, lighting, ventilation, heating and thermal performance of the building construction are all interrelated and cannot be thought of in isolation. In addition, energy conservation will have a major effect on most aspects of the environmental design.[1]

Schools and local authorities make their design decisions in the light of their statutory responsibilities and their own assessments of local priorities and resources. It is hoped that the advice given in this building bulletin will assist this process.

The guidelines are aimed primarily at the designers of new school buildings, but they may also be used as a broad framework for the improvement of existing buildings. They have purposely been kept simple in an effort to be easily accessible both to architects and to engineers. However, references to more detailed standards and sources of further information are quoted at the end of each section. Further detailed advice is currently being prepared as separate building bulletins on lighting design for schools and on acoustics in school buildings.

[1] See also the companion building bulletin 83 *Schools Environmental Assessment Method, SEAM*, which uses energy (carbon dioxide) ratings as part of the overall environmental assessment of both new and existing school buildings. The Stationery Office, 1996, ISBN 0 11 27099206, £14.95.

Section A: Acoustics

General

Acoustic design aims to enable people to hear clearly without distraction. This is achieved by:

- determining appropriate background noise levels and reverberation times for the various activities and room types;
- planning the disposition of 'quiet' and 'noisy' spaces; separating them wherever possible by distance, external areas or neutral 'buffer' spaces such as storerooms or corridors;
- using walls, floors and partitions to provide sound insulation; and
- optimising the acoustical characteristics by considering the room volume, room shape and the acoustic properties of the room surfaces.

The architectural planning should take into consideration the acoustic conditions required. Particular problems arise where insulation between spaces needs to be high and where there is a desire for open plan arrangements containing a number of different activities.

The most serious problems found in schools are due to noise transfer and/or excessive reverberation.

Planning

Tables 1a and 1b give recommended maximum background noise levels and minimum sound insulation levels between rooms for the types of rooms and activities commonly found in schools.

The tables help to assess the compatibility of each activity and should be considered during the early planning stage of a project. The tables can help to determine the layout of the school and the necessary methods of sound insulation.

It will usually be possible to achieve the necessary degree of sound insulation between two activities by interposing a suitable wall. However, if spaces are very diverse in their acoustic requirements, for example a workshop and a lecture theatre, or sports hall and music room, it is seldom practicable to provide the degree of sound insulation necessary by a single wall. Such spaces are better positioned well apart, separated by either an external space or a 'neutral' area such as a store or circulation space to act as a buffer between the two.

Noise control

The noise intruding into the classroom can come from a number of sources, for example, activities in adjacent areas, ventilation equipment and road traffic. During school hours this noise should not normally exceed the levels in Table 1a.

1

The background noise level in general teaching classrooms should not normally be above $40dBL_{Aeq,1hr}$.

When external noise levels are higher than $60dBL_{Aeq,1hr}$, natural ventilation solutions as recommended in Sections C and D may not be appropriate as the ventilation openings also let in noise. However, it is possible to use acoustically attenuated natural ventilation rather than full mechanical ventilation when external noise levels are high but do not exceed $70dBL_{Aeq,1hr}$.

Where external noises are loud and intermittent eg, aircraft and trains, a noise rating representing the highest levels of these events should be used. L_{A1}, the level exceeded for 1% of the time period a room is in use, eg, a lesson, is appropriate. As a general guide, the level from aircraft and trains in teaching classrooms should not normally exceed $55dBL_{A1}$.

Reference should also be made to PPG24 which recommends that, for replacement schools in areas with high aircraft noise, expert consideration of sound insulation measures will be necessary.

Where spaces are mechanically ventilated the background noise from the ventilation system can be used to mask the noise from neighbouring activities. Thus it is beneficial for the minimum background noise level in general teaching classrooms not to fall below $30dBL_{Aeq,1hr}$ (the maximum level should remain at $40dBL_{Aeq,1hr}$ as stated above).

Impact sound insulation may be needed to control noise created by impacts, eg, footsteps on floors. This is an important consideration in upper floors of older buildings which have suspended wooden floors. A good means of control is to reduce the amount of impact energy getting into the floor itself, for example by using a resilient surface, such as carpet or resiliently backed vinyl.

Definition of acoustical terms

$L_{Aeq,T}$ - The equivalent continuous A-weighted sound pressure level. This is a notional steady sound which, over a defined period of time T, would have the same A-weighted acoustic energy as a fluctuating noise, eg, for a 1 hour school lesson this would be denoted $L_{Aeq,1hr}$.

A-weighted sound pressure level, dB(A) - The unit in decibels, generally used for measuring environmental and traffic noise. An A-weighting network can be built into a sound level meter so that dB(A) values can be read directly from the meter. The weighting is based on the frequency response of the human ear and has been found to correlate well with human subjective responses to various sounds. It is worth noting that an increase or decrease of approximately 10dB(A) corresponds to a subjective doubling or halving of the loudness of a noise, while a change of 2 to 3dB(A) is subjectively just perceptible.

Decibel, dB - The decibel is a unit of sound level using a logarithmic scale.

Reverberation - The persistence of sound within a space after the source has ceased.

Reverberation time (RT) - The time in seconds required for a sound to decay to inaudibility after the source ceases; strictly, the time in seconds for the sound level to decay 60dB (The mid-frequency value of RT is the mean of the values in the octaves centred on 500Hz and 1000Hz).

Room type/activity	Activity noise level	Background Noise Level	
	General category	Tolerance level General category	Maximum background noise level from adjacent areas, ventilation and traffic noise $L_{Aeq,1hr}$ (dB)
Music rooms:			
Teaching, listening audio	High	Low	30
Music practice/group rooms	High	Low	30
Ensemble playing	High	Low	30
Recording/control room	High	Low	25
General teaching, seminar and tutorial rooms and classbases	Average	Medium	40
Science laboratories	Average	Medium	40
Language laboratories	Average	Low	35
Commerce and typing	Average	Medium	40
Lecture rooms	Average	Low	35
Drama, play reading and acting	High	Low	30
Assembly/multi-purpose halls[1]	High	Low	35
Audio-visual rooms	Average	Low	35
Libraries	Low - Average	Low	40
Metalwork/woodwork	High	Medium	45
Resource/light craft and practical	High	Medium	45
Individual study	Low	Low	35
Administration offices	Average	Medium	40
Staff rooms	Average	Medium	40
Medical rooms	Average	Medium	40
Withdrawal, remedial work	Low	Low	35
Teacher preparation	Low	Low	35
Interviewing/counselling	Low	Low	35
Indoor sports	High	High	50
Corridors and stairwells	High	High	50
Coats and changing areas	High	High	50
Toilets	Average	High	50
Indoor swimming pools	High	High	50
Dining rooms	High	High	50
Kitchens	High	High	50
Plant rooms	High	High	65

TABLE 1a:
Recommended acoustic standards : Background Noise Level

[1] Halls (especially in primary schools) are multi-functional spaces used for PE, drama, music and assembly. Larger halls are used for performing plays and concerts. Halls are also used for examinations.

Box 1: Relationships between different descriptors of sound insulation

Sound insulation can be described in terms of a Sound Reduction Index, symbol R. It is often averaged over the key part of the audible spectrum and expressed as a single figure value, either R_w (weighted index) or R_m (mean index). The Sound Reduction Index of a construction is normally measured under laboratory conditions and is often quoted in manufacturers' catalogues. It is a property of the construction and is independent of its area and the receiving room reverberation time.

In actual buildings it is appropriate to measure the Sound Level Difference that can be achieved between two rooms, symbol D, or D_w for weighted value. D includes sound transmission via all paths between one room to another, ie, the direct path and flanking paths, and it is representative of the sound insulation achievable in practice. A value of D_w is commonly quoted in standards eg, BS8233: 1987 and Part E of the Building Regulations. D_w is the sound insulation descriptor adopted in Table 1b.

Section A: Acoustics

Table 1b:
Recommended acoustic standards : Sound insulation

[2] Sound insulation below these levels is not recommended because of possible future change of use.

[3] Locating rooms with noisy activities adjacent to rooms with a low noise tolerance should be avoided.
If inevitable, to achieve 52dB, a heavy masonry construction or equivalent will be necessary, eg, 200mm dense concrete blockwork walls. To achieve 58dB a heavy masonry cavity construction with flexible wall ties will be necessary - specialist advice should be sought.

		Minimum sound insulation		
		D_w		
Tolerance level in receiving room	High	38 *(48)	28 *(38)	28[2] *(38)[2]
	Medium	48 *(55)	38 *(48)	28 *(38)
	Low	52[3] *(58)[3]	48 *(55)	38 *(48)
		High	Average	Low

Activity noise level in adjacent space

*Values in brackets are for specialist rooms for teaching the hearing impaired. (See page 7)

Note: Where a room is used for more than one purpose eg, a classroom to be used for music teaching, the higher sound insulation value should be used.

Figure 1:
Optimum reverberation times at 'mid-frequencies' for speech and music related to room volume for unoccupied spaces

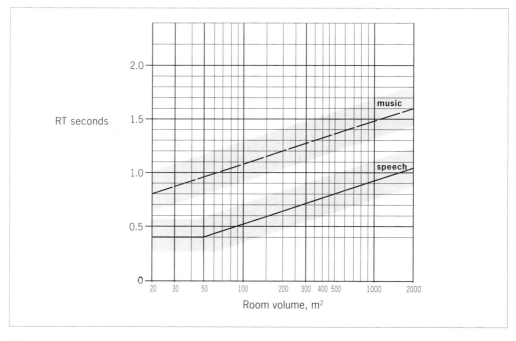

Figure 2:
Rooms specifically for music; recommended percentage increase in reverberation times at lower frequencies

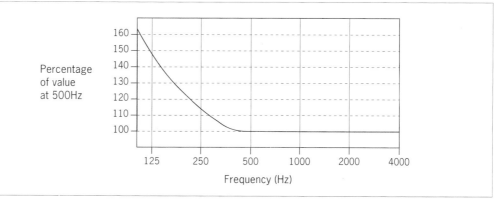

Reverberation time, RT

The reverberation time of a space affects the balance between clarity and reverberance with which a sound is heard. The higher the value of RT the longer the sound takes to decay which shifts the balance from clarity towards reverberance.

Music activities generally benefit from a longer RT than speech. Figure 1 can be used to set the room volume to provide a reverberation time suitable for either music or speech.

Rooms with low acoustic absorption and long reverberation times can suffer from high ambient noise levels when many people try to speak at the same time. There is a tendency for people to increase their voice level to make themselves heard which exacerbates the situation. This is a common feature of school dining rooms and design technology workshops.

Recommended reverberation times for these types of spaces are included in Table 2.

The location of acoustic absorption within a room is also important. For example, classrooms can benefit from having absorbent material on the rear wall but the central ceiling area should be hard and acoustically reflective to allow the teacher's voice to be reflected to all the pupils.

Halls are often used for both speech and music and therefore the reverberation time selected will have to be a compromise to allow for both uses. A good alternative may be to select a reverberation time suitable for music and then reduce the reverberation time for speech by using moveable drapes.

Table 2 gives a range of suitable values for RT for the average sizes of various room types.

Table 2:
Recommended reverberation times for unoccupied spaces

Type of room	Approximate size		Recommended unoccupied mid-frequency [4] Reverberation Time (seconds)
	Area (m²)	Height (m)	
Primary schools:			
Classroom or class-base	30 - 65	2.4 - 3.0	0.5 - 0.8
Library	12 - 70	2.4 - 3.0	0.5 - 0.8
Music & drama studio/AV room	30 - 80	2.4 - 4.0	0.8 - 1.2
Hall (assembly/PE/movement)	80 - 200	3.7 - 6.0	0.8 - 1.2
Dining Rooms	80 - 200	2.4 - 3.2	0.5 - 0.8
Hall (music, drama, PE, AVA, assembly)	80 - 200	3.7 - 6.0	0.8 - 1.4
Swimming pool	65 - 120	3.7 - 6.0	< 2.0
Kitchens	65 - 120	2.7 - 4.0	1.5
Secondary schools:			
General teaching classroom	50 - 70	2.4 - 3.0	0.5 - 0.8
Small practical spaces: science, IT, business studies,	70 - 110	2.4 - 3.0	0.5 - 0.8
Large practical spaces: art, metalwork, woodwork, multi-materials, textiles, electronics, food technology	80 - 135	2.7 - 3.0	0.5 - 0.8
Library	90 - 300	2.4 - 3.0	0.5 - 1.0
Hall (assembly/rehearsal)	250 - 550	3.7 - 7.6	1.0 - 1.4
Dining rooms	250 - 550	3.7 - 7.6	0.5 - 0.8
Gymnasium/PE	250 - 550	5.0 - 6.0	1.0 - 1.5
Dance studio	150	2.7 - 4.0	0.8 - 1.2
Drama studio	80 - 120	3.7 - 7.0	0.9 - 1.1
Swimming pool	100 - 500	3.0 - 6.0	<2.0
Music rooms:			
Music classroom/recital room	54 - 91	2.7 - 3.5	1.0 - 1.2
Ensemble rooms	16 - 50	2.7 - 4.0	0.8 - 1.2
Small teaching/practice/group room	6 - 10	2.7 - 3.0	0.4 - 0.8
Recording/control room	8 - 15	2.4 - 3.0	0.3 - 0.8

[4] Mid-frequency RT is the mean of the 500Hz and 1000Hz octave band values.

Open plan areas

In open plan areas it is essential to provide good speech intelligibility at short distances (up to 5m) and to secure freedom from aural distraction by more distant sound sources and by background noise. Some degree of privacy is also desirable.

This can be difficult to achieve in practice and there have been many instances of distraction and disturbance between class groups in open plan areas.

To realise the limited acoustic potential of open plan areas, a carpeted floor is recommended together with an acoustically absorbent ceiling. In addition, acoustically absorbent screens, of typical height 1.7m, should be interposed between class groups.

A major improvement in the use of open plan areas can be obtained by installing full height moveable walls which, if fitted with seals, can provide a moderate degree of sound insulation between the divided spaces.

Art, design and technology spaces

There is often a desire to integrate the various disciplines of these subject areas with insufficient consideration of direct and indirect noise transfer problems.

Areas containing woodwork and metalwork or other noisy machinery can produce high noise levels and it is advisable to locate these in spaces separated from quieter activities such as class instruction in art and design.

Music rooms

Music rooms can be the most difficult part of the acoustic design of a school and it is important to establish the user's expectations of the acoustic performance of the spaces. The main problems encountered are noise transfer between spaces, unsuitable reverberation times, flutter echoes[5] and standing waves[6], and excessively high noise levels producing stress and complaints from teaching staff.

There are four basic requirements for good listening conditions:

- the background noise level should be sufficiently low to permit the full dynamic range of the music to be heard;
- the reverberation time should be suitable for the activity and should be constant over the mid to high frequency range. An increase of up to 50% is permissible at bass frequencies as indicated in Figure 2;
- there should be freedom from echoes, flutter echoes, standing waves, focusing and any other acoustic effects which confuse or distort the sound;
- the sound should be distributed uniformly throughout the room, both in the performance and listening areas. It is beneficial in this respect to model large flat wall surfaces to a depth of 0.3m or more. An alternative is to use large convex surfaces, in plan and section.

Table 1b recommends a minimum D_w of 52dB between music rooms. It is beneficial to increase this to 55dB or higher when the background noise level is low, ie, below $30dBL_{Aeq,1hr}$. This can occur in naturally ventilated rooms on quiet sites where the background noise is too low to provide useful masking of distracting noise from adjacent rooms.

Design of acoustics for pupils with hearing and visual impairments

Lighting and acoustic criteria are very important both to the hearing impaired and to the visually impaired. If one sensory channel is impaired more reliance is placed on the unimpaired sensory channel, for example, the use of aural cues by the visually impaired and lip-reading by the hearing impaired. (See also advice on lighting on page 12).

It is incorrect to assume that school acoustics do not matter if the pupils are

[5] A flutter echo is an audible perception of sound reflecting repeatedly to and fro between parallel walls.

[6] A standing wave is caused by interference between two waves travelling in opposite directions, often between parallel walls. Sound pressure maxima and minima are formed which can colour the original sound.

severely hearing impaired; even profoundly hearing impaired pupils can detect changes in the intonation and syllabic content of speech. Hearing impaired pupils may use residual hearing as one of a number of means of communication available to them and good acoustic conditions are required to give pupils the best opportunity to optimise their use of residual hearing.

Whilst people with no hearing impairment can filter out unimportant background noise so that they can hear the sounds which they are interested in (the 'Cocktail Party Effect'), this is very difficult for the hearing impaired. In all teaching areas, therefore, low background noise levels are beneficial for the hearing impaired.

High levels of intrusive noise increase the background noise and hence reduce pupils' ability to discriminate between speech and noise. Careful space planning should be carried out to locate noise producing spaces away from noise sensitive spaces where possible, to reduce the performance requirements of sound insulating constructions.

Staff or pupils with hearing impairments may require special facilities such as hearing aids, radio aids and induction loops. Invasive noise such as mechanical ventilation or the hum of fluorescent lights can interfere with these. As hearing aids amplify unwanted sound as well as speech, control of reverberant noise levels in teaching rooms is important for the hearing impaired. Controlled reverberation times aid good speech intelligibility.

Specialist accommodation for pupils with hearing impairments

The following acoustic criteria are recommended for special schools and special units in mainstream schools designed for teaching the hearing impaired.

Background noise

In order to achieve good speech signal/noise level ratios and thus increase the pupils' ability to make the most of their residual hearing, it is proposed that maximum background noise levels in all rooms for teaching the hearing impaired should be at least 10dB lower than the standards quoted in Table 1a on page 3 for the equivalent classrooms in mainstream schools.

Many hearing impaired people make use of frequencies below 500Hz to obtain information from speech. Therefore care should be especially taken to minimise low frequency background noise levels.

Sound insulation

Table 1a also recommends Activity Noise Level and Tolerance Level categories for various teaching spaces. In rooms for teaching the hearing impaired, these categories are not changed but the recommended standards for sound insulation have been adjusted to reflect the lower recommended background noise levels. The adjusted figures are shown in brackets in Table 1b on page 4, underneath the figures for mainstream accommodation.

Reverberation time

In rooms for teaching the hearing impaired, good speech intelligibility is essential. Long reverberation times can lead to poor speech intelligibility and high reverberant ambient noise levels which make speech discrimination difficult. Long reverberation times should be avoided.

It is recommended that the unoccupied mid-frequency reverberation time in classrooms for teaching the hearing impaired is between 0.3 and 0.6 seconds.

Specialist audiology facilities may be required including an audiometry test room. The acoustic requirements of this space are beyond the scope of this document.

Bibliography

Miller, J., *Design standards for the sound insulation of music practice rooms.* Acoustics Bulletin of the Institute of Acoustics, Vol. 18, No. 6, Nov/Dec 1993, pp 54-58.

Sound control for homes. BRE and CIRIA, 1993. ISBN 0 85125 55900.

Parkin, P.H., Humphreys, H.R. and Cowell, J.R. *Acoustics, Noise and Buildings,* Fourth Edition. Faber and Faber, London, 1979.

Noise Control in Building Services. Fry, A. (ed.), Sound Research Laboratories Ltd. Pergamon Press, Oxford, 1988. ISBN 0 08 034067 9.

Lord, P. and Templeton, D. *Detailing for Acoustics,* Third Edition. E. & F. N. Spon, London, 1996. ISBN 0 419 20210 2.

Templeton, D.W. and Saunders, D. *Acoustic Design.* Architectural Press, London, 1987. ISBN 0 85139 018 8.

Policy Planning Guide, PPG24, Department of the Environment, 1996.

BRE/BRS Building Digests as relevant.

BS8233: 1987: *Code of Practice for Sound insulation and noise reduction for buildings,* Section 3, Part 9, Educational buildings.

BS5821: Part 1: 1984 (ISO 717/1 - 1982): *Method for rating the airborne sound insulation in buildings and of interior building elements.*

BS2750: Part 4: 1980 (ISO/IV - 1978): *Field measurements of airborne sound insulation between rooms.*

New DfEE Building Bulletin *Acoustic Design of Schools* to be published shortly.

Section B: Lighting

References
[1] CIBSE *Code for Interior Lighting*, 1994, ISBN 0 900953 64 0.

The School Premises Regulations

(1) Each room or other space in a school building -
   (a) shall have lighting appropriate to its normal use; and
   (b) shall satisfy the requirements of paragraphs (2) to (4)

(2) Subject to paragraph (3), the maintained illuminance of teaching accommodation shall be not less than 300 lux on the working plane.

(3) In teaching accommodation where visually demanding tasks are carried out provision shall be made for a maintained illuminance of not less than 500 lux on the working plane.

(4) The glare index shall be limited to no more than 19.

Note: Since 1994, recommended illuminance is described as maintained illuminance, and is defined in the CIBSE Code for Interior Lighting, 1994:[1] 'The average illuminance over the reference surface at the time maintenance has to be carried out by replacing lamps and/or cleaning the equipment and room surfaces'.

Recommended constructional standards

Priority should be given to daylight as the main source of light in working areas, except in special circumstances. Wherever possible a daylit space should have an average daylight factor of 4–5%.

The uniformity ratio (minimum/average maintained illuminance) of the electric lighting in teaching areas should be not less than 0.8 over the task area.[1]

Teaching spaces should have views out except in special circumstances. A minimum glazed area of 20% of the internal elevation of the exterior wall is recommended to provide adequate views out.

A maintained illuminance at floor level in the range 80 - 120 lux is recommended for stairs and corridors.

Entrance halls, lobbies and waiting rooms require a higher illuminance in the range 175 - 250 lux on the appropriate plane.

The type of luminaires should be chosen to give an average initial circuit luminous efficacy of 65 lumens/circuit watt for the fixed lighting equipment within the building, excluding track-mounted luminaires and emergency lighting.

Introduction

A successful lighting installation is one that satisfies a number of different criteria shown in the following lighting design framework. The criteria will not have equal weight but all should be considered to arrive at the best solution.

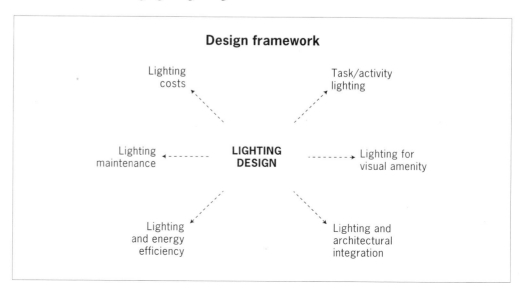

Design framework

Lighting costs — Task/activity lighting — Lighting maintenance — **LIGHTING DESIGN** — Lighting for visual amenity — Lighting and energy efficiency — Lighting and architectural integration

Task/activity lighting

Here the designer needs to examine the functional requirements of the particular space. It is necessary to consider the amount of light and the type of lighting required to ensure that the users of the space can carry out their particular tasks without visual difficulty and in a comfortable visual environment. Hence the first consideration here is to analyse the activity requirements for particular spaces.

It may be necessary to provide flexibility in the lighting to allow for a variety of ativities. Local task lighting can be very useful for specific tasks. Safety should be considered in choosing the type of local task light, eg, surface temperature of the fitting.

An increase in the size or contrast of the task detail, eg, typeface may be an alternative to higher levels of illuminance particularly for the visually impaired.

Lighting for visual amenity

This aspect of lighting addresses the appearance of the lit scene, the aim being to create a 'light' environment that is visually interesting and pleasant. This means creating a light pattern that has luminance variation and a sensitive use of surface colour.

Lighting and architectural integration

It is important that a lighting installation, both natural and electric, appears an integrated part of the architecture. This will apply both to the lighting elements (windows and luminaires) and the light patterns they produce.

Lighting and energy efficiency

This will mean making the maximum use of daylight, using electric light to complement daylight, and using energy-efficient electric lighting that only operates when it is required. This last point can be covered by the positions of the control switches, by the organisation of the lighting circuits to relate to the daylight distribution and to the use of the space. Automatic controls can provide useful energy savings but it is essential that any controls are user friendly, ie, they do not hinder the use of the space.[2]

The type of luminaires should be chosen to give an average initial circuit luminous efficacy of 65 lumens/circuit watt for the fixed lighting equipment within the building. Both emergency lighting systems and equipment which is not fixed, eg, track-mounted luminaires are excluded from this figure.[3]

Lighting maintenance

All lighting will deteriorate with time due to dirt build-up on the lamps and luminaires, on the windows, on the reflecting surfaces of the space and also due to lamp light output depreciation. The designer will need to consider these matters in making decisions to ensure that the lit environment is satisfactory over the whole maintenance cycle. This will mean liaising with the client to plan a suitable maintenance programme.

It is worth remembering that use of a wide range of different lamp types makes subsequent replacement more complicated.

All lighting elements including windows should be easy to clean and maintain.

Lighting costs

Both capital costs and running costs will need to be considered to ensure a cost effective design. This is particularly important if the two costs are to be met by different budgets.

References
[2] BRE Information Paper IP6/96, *People and lighting controls.*

[3] Approved Document L (*Conservation of fuel and power*) in support of the Building Regulations, Department of the Environment and Welsh Office, Section 2.4.2 Lighting, HMSO 1995, ISBN 0 11 752933 8, £11.

Design criteria

Daylighting

Natural light should be the prime means of lighting during daylight hours. A space is likely to be considered well lit if there is an average daylight factor of 4-5%. For the daylight illuminance to be adequate for the task, it will be necessary to achieve a level of not less than 300 lux, and for particularly demanding tasks not less than 500 lux. When this cannot be achieved, the daylight will need to be supplemented by electric light. Light exterior surfaces can sometimes be used to increase reflected light.

The design of the fenestration should relate to the layout and activities planned for the internal space, eg, to avoid silhouetting effects and excessive contrasts in brightness.

Discomfort and disability glare are possible from daylight, and in particular from direct sunlight. This potential problem can often be solved by careful design of the fenestration to minimise glare. Alternatively, adjustable blinds can be provided to screen the glare source when necessary. Blinds can also improve the thermal environment by reducing heat gains. Although they are more expensive than internal blinds, external blinds are more effective in preventing solar heat gain. Internal blinds are often difficult to maintain and are a source of noise when windows are open.

Windows are important as they provide natural variation of light through the day and external visual interest. For the window area to be adequate for this purpose, it is recommended that a minimum glazed area of 20% of the internal elevation of the exterior wall is provided.

Windows, in addition to being treated as a lighting source and providing a view out, need to be considered in terms of other environmental factors, eg, the thermal and acoustic performance together with the energy efficiency of the building.

Electric lighting

The electric lighting installation will need to meet all the requirements shown in the design framework.

In terms of task lighting, for most school tasks, a maintained illuminance of 300 lux will be appropriate. If the task is particularly demanding, eg, the task detail content is small or it has a low contrast, then a value of not less than 500 lux will be necessary: in some situations, this can be provided by a local supplement to the general lighting.

A maintained illuminance at floor level in the range 80 - 120 lux is recommended for stairs and corridors. Entrance halls, lobbies and waiting rooms require a higher illuminance in the range 175 - 250 lux at an appropriate level. Reception areas should be lit to a level in the range 250 - 350 lux on the working plane.

In terms of avoiding discomfort glare, where a regular array of luminaires is used, the Glare Index shall be limited to no more than 19.[4] It will also be important to avoid visual discomfort from individual luminaires and from reflected images, on computer screens in particular.

An additional consideration on visual comfort is the avoidance of subliminal lamp flicker. This can be important as it can induce epileptic fits in susceptible pupils (see page 14). It can be minimised by the use of high frequency control gear or using more than one phase of a three phase supply in a lead-lag arrangement. The stroboscopic effect of lamp flicker must be addressed in areas with rotating machinery, eg, circular saws.

Colour appreciation is an important part of learning, and hence it is necessary to use electric light sources that present colours accurately, particularly in art and design rooms. Good colour rendering is not now very expensive to achieve. In this respect, lamps with a CIE Colour Rendering Index (R_a) of not less than 80 are recommended. With regard to colour appearance, lamps with a Warm to Intermediate classification (Correlated Colour Temperature 2800°K - 4000°K) should be used.

References
[4] CIBSE Technical Memorandum 10, *The Calculation of Glare Indices*, 1985.

Switching arrangements should facilitate shared use of spaces where appropriate.

Combined daylighting and electric lighting

A specially designed supplement of electric lighting should be provided when the daylighting recommendations cannot be achieved throughout a space. In addition to providing a combined illuminance for the task or activities being undertaken, a satisfactory appearance should be obtained by a balance of brightness throughout the space to cope with relatively bright windows. This can be achieved by preferential lighting, and particularly wall lighting in areas remote from the window.

In these spaces, it is recommended that the colour appearance of the lamps used should be in the Intermediate classification with a Correlated Colour Temperature of about 4000°K.

Lighting quality

In terms of the appearance of the lighting, both natural and electric, it will be necessary to consider the overall light pattern in terms of 'apparent lightness', ie, the overall lightness of the space and 'visual interest', ie, a term relating to the degree of non-uniformity in the light pattern. The bright parts can frequently be the highlight areas used for display purposes.

Another aspect that is important is the integration of the lighting (equipment and light pattern) with the surface colours and textures and the overall architecture.

These are attributes which recent research has shown are important for the users of a space, but because they are subjective, they cannot easily be quantified.

However, for the space to have an acceptable 'apparent lightness', it will be necessary to use relatively high surface reflectances, ie, wall finish reflectance not less than 0.6 with a ceiling finish reflectance not less than 0.7 and a floor reflectance as high as is practicable. Glossy finishes to ceilings and walls should be avoided to minimise confusing reflections and glare. (Note: since it is common practice for teachers to use the wall surfaces for display, a lower average wall reflectance value, eg, 0.3 - 0.5 will need to be used for calculations, depending on the wall finish and the amount of display material.)

The choice of surface colours is important as it affects not only the surface reflectances but also the overall visual impression.

External lighting

Exterior lighting may be needed for:

- roadway/pathway lighting;
- floodlighting of the building at night;
- floodlighting of outdoor sports.

Attention is needed to avoid light trespass which causes a nuisance to people and dwellings in the neighbourhood.

Light pollution which affects the local environment and atmosphere should also be avoided.

Light trespass can be controlled by suitable selection of the light distribution of luminaires to avoid 'spill light' and by careful aiming of floodlights with the use of shields if necessary.

Generally the intensity of a floodlight beam diminishes away from the centre. In order to control glare from light it is often necessary to refer to the beam angle within which the intensity of the light falls to one tenth of the peak intensity of the beam.

To prevent light pollution, the light defined by this beam angle must fall within an angle of 70° from the downward vertical. These are called full-cut lanterns and usually require flat glasses.

To achieve the correct uniformity in car parks or playing fields higher columns or closer spacing may be required.

While there is no legislation concerning light pollution it has become a major planning issue with Local Authorities especially concerning effects on local residents. Planning Departments often turn down proposals which would introduce major new light sources into areas with only low to moderate levels of illumination and which would create substantial sky glow.

External lighting without automatic control is not energy efficient. Some form of automatic control should be provided.

Control can be by photocells and timeswitches or passive infra-red detectors. The types of luminaires and controls available are described in detail in DfEE Building Bulletin 78.[5]

Emergency lighting

The purpose of emergency lighting is to provide sufficient illumination, in the event of a failure of the electricity supply to the normal electric lighting, to enable the building to be evacuated quickly and safely and to control processes, machinery, etc, securely.

In schools, emergency lighting is only usually provided in areas accessible to the general public during the evenings. These include halls and drama spaces used for performances. Emergency lighting is not usually provided on escape routes, except from public areas, as the children are generally familiar with the buildings and there is only a relatively small part of the school year during the hours of darkness.

Exceptions where emergency lighting might be considered are upstairs escape corridors, escape stairways, corridors without any windows and areas with dangerous machinery.

It is recommended that for halls, gymnasia and other areas used by the public during the hours of darkness the emergency lighting should be of the maintained type. Where part of the premises is licensed it will be necessary to seek the advice and guidance of the Local Fire Authority.

Emergency Lighting should reveal safe passageways out of the building together with the fire alarm call points, the fire fighting equipment, escape signs and any permanent hazards along the escape routes such as changes of direction or stairs. Further detail is given in the Building Bulletin *Lighting Design for Schools.* [6]

Lighting for pupils with visual and hearing impairments

Lighting and acoustic criteria are very important both to the hearing impaired and to the visually impaired. If one sensory channel is impaired more reliance is placed on the unimpaired sensory channel. For example, the use of aural cues by the visually impaired and lip-reading by the hearing impaired. (See also advice on acoustics on page 6.)

The design of specialist accommodation for the visually impaired is beyond the scope of this document and specialist advice should be sought.[7&8] However, there are design choices that should be considered for all schools. Many of the low cost or no cost measures can be applied to existing buildings such as the choice of decor, tactile surfaces and types of luminaires. For a detailed description of possible measures see *Building Sight* published by the RNIB.[9]

Other measures, such as providing or facilitating the use of visual aids can be considered as necessary. There is no single solution and what may assist one person may well not assist another. The following notes are offered as a general guide and should help in the majority of cases.

Visual impairment can be put into two broad classifications.

Field defects

Firstly, there are conditions where what is seen is seen clearly but the visual field is restricted. It may be that only the central part of the field is seen (tunnel vision). In this case mobility would be impaired although reading and the ability to do fine work would be largely unaffected.

References

[5] DfEE Building Bulletin 78, Security Lighting, HMSO 1993, ISBN 0 11 270822 6

[6] New DfEE *Building Bulletin Lighting Design for Schools* to be published shortly.

[7] RNIB/GBDA Joint Mobility Unit, 224 Great Portland Street, London, W1N 6AA, Tel: 0171 388 1266, Fax: 0171 388 3160.

[8] The Partially Sighted Society, 62 Salusbury Road, London, NW6 6NS, Tel: 0171 372 1551.

[9] *Building Sight*, Peter Barker, Jon Barrick, Rod Wilson, RNIB, ISBN 011 701 993 3, HMSO, 1995, £35.

The converse, loss of central vision, would mean that movement could be made in safety but the ability to perform detailed tasks such as reading or sewing would be extremely difficult if not impossible.

In all types of field defect the quantity of task illumination is generally unimportant providing normal recommendations are followed. Glare should be avoided (see section on loss of acuity below) and decor can help rapid orientation (see section on use of colour below).

Loss of acuity

The other main condition is a loss of acuity or a blurring of vision. The extent of the blurring varies widely and some pupils may have to bring objects and print extremely close to their eyes to see best. There may also be an associated loss of colour vision.

Large print will, and higher illuminance may, be of assistance depending upon the cause of the loss of acuity. Many schools now have the facility to produce their own reading material and the use of a san serif font of at least 14pt size can be a useful aid.

The effects of low acuity can be aggravated by glare, and this should be avoided. A 'white' board on a dark coloured wall can be a glare source whereas a traditional 'blackboard' would not. Similarly, a view of a daylit scene through a window can be a disabling glare source.

Both loss of field and loss of acuity can occur together and, the particular difficulties which people with visual impairment experience, and their responses to light and other environmental features, can vary widely.

The use of higher than normal task illuminances can be of help to those whose acuity can be improved by the contraction of the iris, producing a greater depth of field. In some cases, however, such as those with central cornea opacities, the iris needs to be dilated so that the student sees 'around' the opacity. In such a case more light will aggravate, not relieve, the condition.

Positioning

Students with visual impairment should be seated where they can best see the work in progress. This may mean a position outside the normal arrangement, eg, immediately in front of the teacher or board.

It is also important that any visual aids are readily available for use. These may range from hand-held or stand mounted optical magnifiers to CCTV magnifiers. Local task lighting may also be used as an aid.

It may be necessary to allow the student to change position within the teaching space to accommodate access to an electrical supply, cope with excess daylight or use any other aid that is available.

Use of colour

Colour and contrast are particularly important to the visually impaired and the hearing impaired.[9] For example, downlighters in reception or teaching areas produce harsh shadows which obstruct lip reading.

Careful use of the colour scheme can help pupils recognise and identify a location. It can be more important than an elaborate lighting installation.

Some visual impairments involve a degree of colour blindness and it is important that contrast should be introduced in luminance and not just colour. For example, pale green and pale cream may be clearly distinguished by the normally sighted but be seen as a single shade of grey even by some pupils where an impairment has not been identified.

Contrast in the decor should be used to aid orientation within a space. For instance, using a darker colour for the architrave around a door will aid location of the door and a handle which clearly contrasts with the surface of the door will indicate which way it swings.

While in some spaces orientation may be established by the furniture arrangement or by windows during daylight hours, in others it can be aided by making one wall distinctly

Section B: Lighting

References
[1] CIBSE *Code for Interior Lighting*, 1994, ISBN 0 900953 64 0.

[2] BRE Information Paper IP6/96, *People and lighting controls*.

[3] Approved Document L *(Conservation of fuel and power)* in support of the Building Regulations, Department of the Environment and Welsh Office, Section 2.4.2 Lighting, HMSO 1995, ISBN 0 11 752933 8, £11.

[4] CIBSE Technical Memorandum 10, *The Calculation of Glare Indices*, 1985.

[5] DfEE Building Bulletin 78, Security Lighting, HMSO 1993, ISBN 0 11 270822 6

[6] New DfEE *Building Bulletin Lighting Design for Schools* to be published shortly.

[7] RNIB/GBDA Joint Mobility Unit, 224 Great Portland Street, London, W1N 6AA, Tel: 0171 388 1266, Fax: 0171 388 3160.

[8] The Partially Sighted Society, 62 Salusbury Road, London, NW6 6NS, Tel: 0171 372 1551.

[9] *Building Sight*, Peter Barker, Jon Barrick, Rod Wilson, RNIB, ISBN 011 701 993 3, HMSO, 1995, £35.

CIBSE *Lighting Guide, Lighting for Visual Display Units*, LG3: Revised 1996.

CIBSE Lighting Guide, *The visual environment in lecture, teaching and conference rooms*, LG5:1991.

CIBSE Applications Manual, *Window Design*, AM2: 1987, ISBN 0 900953 33 0.

Energy efficient lighting in schools, BRECSU-OPET, Building Research Establishment.

different, perhaps by the addition of a large clock or a change in colour. Whatever method is used, it is best adhered to throughout the building, ie, the different wall is always to the same side of the main exit from the space.

High gloss finishes should be used with care as they can appear as glare sources when they reflect bright lights such as sunlight. In general, eggshell finishes are to be preferred as some directional reflection is desirable rather than dead matt surfaces which may be difficult to place precisely.

Changes in the tactile qualities of surfaces can also be useful to reinforce visual contrasts. They are most important in schools for the blind.

Daylight

Generally schools should be designed with daylight as the principal light source. The window wall should be light in colour, to reduce contrast with the outdoor scene, and window reveals may be splayed to increase the apparent size of the glazing.

Sunlight can be either a help or a hindrance, depending on the type of visual impairment, and some means of controlling the quantity should be provided. Traditionally this has been by means of blinds. The design of fenestration in circulation spaces should minimise glare hazards.

Large areas of glazing can be hazardous to the visually impaired unless they can be clearly seen. To avoid accidents they can be marked with a contrasting feature at eye level. This should be visible in low light levels.

In the UK the greatest problems, both visual and thermal, are caused by low altitude sunlight at either end of the school day. Any solar shading device, including those for rooflights must, therefore, be readily adjustable to cater for a range of conditions. Adjustment of solar shading should preferably be at the discretion of the students and not the teaching staff who may not fully appreciate the visual difficulties of the students.

Electric light

The control of glare from overhead lighting is particularly important to students with a visual impairment.

High frequency electronic ballasts for fluorescent lamps are to be preferred as they avoid subliminal flicker and also the annoying visible flicker that conventionally ballasted lamps can demostrate at the end of their life. If high frequency ballasts are used, consideration should be given to using a regulated version which can be dimmed to allow the illuminance level to be adjusted to suit the individual as well as to save energy. The additional cost for this is usually modest.

It is not normally economic to install more than the recommended illuminances on the off-chance that they will be useful some day to a hypothetical visually impaired student. Additional illuminance can often be readily supplied when the need arises from local task lighting luminaires.

Escape routes should be clearly identified and alarm systems (visual and acoustic) should be adequate.

Summary of main points on lighting for pupils with visual impairments

- Provide contrast in the decor to aid the location of doors and their handles, switches and socket outlets, changes in direction in corridors, changes in floor level, stairs and steps.

- Avoid glare from windows, rooflights and luminaires; either distant or immediately overhead.

- Provide facilities for the use of any visual aids, eg, magnifiers, telescopes, etc.

- Provide additional illumination by adjustable local task lighting as needed.

Section C: Heating and thermal performance

The School Premises Regulations

Heating

(1) Each room or other space in a school building shall have such system of heating, if any, as is appropriate to its normal use.

(2) Any such heating system shall be capable of maintaining in the areas set out in column (1) of the Table below the air temperature set out opposite thereto, in column (2) of that Table, at a height of 0.5m above floor level when the external air temperature is –1°C:

Column 1 Area	Column 2 Temperature
Areas where there is the normal level of physical activity associated with teaching, private study or examinations.	18°C
Areas where there is a lower than normal level of physical activity because of sickness or physical disability including sick rooms and isolation rooms but not other sleeping accommodation.	21°C
Areas where there is a higher than normal level of physical activity (for example arising out of physical education) and washrooms, sleeping accommodation and circulation spaces.	15°C

(3) Each room or other space which has a heating system shall, if the temperature during any period during which it is occupied would otherwise be below that appropriate to its normal use, be heated to a temperature which is so appropriate.

(4) In a special school, nursery school or teaching accommodation used by a nursery class in a school the surface temperature of any radiator, including exposed pipework, which is in a position where it may be touched by a pupil shall not exceed 43°C.

Recommended constructional standards

The heating system should be capable of maintaining the minimum air temperatures quoted in the School Premises Regulations.

The heating system should be provided with frost protection.

During the summer, when the heating system is not in operation, the recommended design temperature for all spaces should be 23°C with a swing of not more than +/– 4°C. It is undesirable for peak air temperatures to exceed 28°C during normal working hours but a higher temperature on 10 days during the summer term is considered a reasonable predictive risk.

The air supply to and discharge of products of combustion from heat producing appliances and the protection of the building from the appliances and their flue pipes and chimneys should comply with Building Regulations, Part J, 1990.

The recommended maximum values of average thermal transmittance coefficients (calculated using the 'Proportional Area Method' used in the Building Regulations, Part L, 1994) are :

	$W/m^2°C$			$W/m^2°C$
Walls	0.4		Roof with a loft space	0.25
Floor	0.4		Doors, windows and rooflights	2.8
Roof	0.3			

Vertical glazed areas (including clerestory or monitor lights) should not normally exceed an average of 40% of the internal elevation of the external wall. However, where a passive solar or daylight design strategy has been adopted the percentage glazing may well exceed 40%. Also in areas prone to breakages due to vandalism the replacement cost may justify the use of single glazing instead of double glazing. In these cases the insulation of the rest of the building fabric should be increased to compensate for the increased heat loss through the glazing.

Horizontal or near horizontal glazing should not normally exceed 20% of the roof area.

Energy conservation

In the design of the thermal environment, due regard should be paid to the need to conserve energy. Particular attention should be paid to the design and orientation of the building so that solar heat gain and energy loss can be optimised.

Thermal conditions

The thermal conditions within educational buildings should be appropriate to the activities and clothing of the occupants. Good control of the heating system is essential not only to maintain comfortable conditions but also to eliminate waste of fuel.

Thermal comfort is achieved when a balance is maintained between the heat produced by the body and the loss of heat to the surroundings. The rate of heat loss is dependent upon the amount of clothing worn and the temperature of the air and surrounding surfaces. In a normal school environment the hourly rate of heat production by the children varies with activity between 70 watts and 100 watts. This heat is lost to the surroundings by the normal processes of convection, conduction, radiation and evaporation. It is therefore necessary for the designer to take account of the functions of spaces and the activities that they contain, and the type of clothing likely to be worn.

Other incidental heat gains (eg, teaching equipment and light fittings) will also contribute heat to the space. Allowing for these and designing suitably responsive controls and heating systems will help to reduce fuel consumption.

Solar gains can be beneficial if careful consideration is given to the design and orientation of the building, but excessive solar gains may lead to overheating. Windows on a south-east facing facade will allow entry of sunlight early in the morning but will avoid direct sunlight during midday and early afternoon when the solar radiation is more intense.

Temperatures in the heating season

The air temperatures quoted in The School Premises Regulations should be maintained during normal hours of occupation throughout the heating season when there is a minimum provision of 3 litres of fresh air per person per second and assuming an external temperature of -1°C. This external temperature is not intended for use in the designing of the heating plant. For sizing of the heating system, Section A2 of the CIBSE guide should be referred to.[1]

Higher air temperatures are often needed in schools for those children with special educational needs who may be more sensitive to the cold.[2]

Excessive vertical temperature gradients should be avoided and the temperature at 2.0m should not exceed that at floor level by more than 3°C.

In some establishments like nursery schools and those for the severely handicapped, it is necessary to prevent children from touching heated surfaces above 43°C by the use of suitable screens or guards.

Multi-purpose spaces should have heating capable of adjustment, so that the space is kept at the temperature required for the activity and not at a higher or lower level than is needed.

Summertime temperatures

An undesirable rise in temperature during warm weather can be caused by uncontrolled incidental and solar heat gains, or by high densities of occupation, eg, in lecture rooms. In these circumstances sufficient natural ventilation is particularly important. Mechanical ventilation may be necessary in some instances to help to control air temperature. Reflective, white or very light roof surfaces reduce the solar heat gain through the roof as well as reducing the thermal stress in the weatherproof covering, but will tend to become less effective without adequate maintenance. Thermal mass and roof insulation also help to reduce this solar gain.

References
[1] CIBSE Guide, Section A2, *Weather and Solar Data.*

[2] DfEE Building Bulletin 77, *Designing for pupils with special educational needs: special schools*, HMSO 1992, ISBN 0 11 270796 3, £14.95

Excessive solar heat gain through windows can be minimised by appropriate orientation and by the use of 'brise soleil' structural shading, louvres, blinds and curtains. Shading the glass from the outside is the most effective method of control, but weather conditions in this country fluctuate in a way that calls for careful design of sun shading devices so as not to unduly impair the daylighting of a classroom.

Storage temperatures for food, including lunch boxes needs to be considered.

Thermal insulation

Adequate thermal insulation of roof and walls is necessary not only to reduce heat loss but also to make the internal surfaces of the building warmer and to reduce the risk of condensation.

In addition to insulating the building fabric it is important also to insulate adequately all heating mains including valves, and hot water storage tanks. Thermal insulation of vessels, pipes and ducts according to Part L of the Building Regulations is sufficient.[3]

Temperatures greater than normal will occur at ceiling level in buildings with spaces higher than 3m. In these cases increased roof insulation should be considered. Recirculation of warm air to low level using 'punka' or ducted fans may be worthwhile.

U-values

U-values should be calculated using the proportional area method of Part L of the Building Regulations which takes account of thermal bridging. Table 7 of Part L gives indicative values of U-values for windows, rooflights and doors which may be used. Thermal bridging around openings should also be reduced by compliance with Part L.

Where higher percentage glazed areas are required than recommended, double glazing should be used and the fabric insulation should be increased to compensate for the increased heat loss through the windows using one of the calculation methods listed in Part L.

Double glazing reduces the risk of condensation and improves comfort conditions. However the replacement cost of broken units can be prohibitive in areas prone to breakages.

Every opportunity should be taken to improve the thermal insulation of existing buildings so that they are as close as reasonably possible to the standards for new buildings.

Heating installation

The installation should be capable of achieving the temperatures recommended in The School Premises Regulations. Occupancy and solar gains may provide additional heat. However, the heating system must be responsive enough to adjust to these gains.

The choice of heat emitter is an important design decision. It will depend on the thermal mass of the construction, the use of solar heat gain, the type of ventilation and the level of fabric insulation, etc.

Radiators are generally the most suitable for teaching spaces. In some primary schools where extensive use is made of the floor hot water underfloor heating is preferred. This is not appropriate where the floor area is likely to be covered, eg, with insulating mats or 'bleacher' seating.

Large infrequently used spaces such as halls can benefit from a faster response and fan convectors or low temperature radiant panels are often used. Low temperature radiant panels can be fixed to ceilings rather than taking up valuable wall space. However, they can produce thermal stratification and this should be considered at the design stage. Underfloor heating is sometimes used in halls to keep walls clear and to avoid background noise.

Wall space is often a priority in schools and fan convectors can then be used in preference to radiators. However, it should be remembered that fan convectors have a high maintenance cost. The background noise level of the fan convectors should not be too high for the planned activities.

References
[3] Approved Document L (*Conservation of fuel and power*) in support of the Building Regulations, Department of the Environment and Welsh Office, 1994, ISBN 0 11 752933 8, £11.

The shorter the heat-up period prior to occupation, the less fuel is used. This is the case particularly in buildings with intermittent occupancy such as schools. To achieve an effective and efficient heat-up, optimum start controls should generally be provided. Similarly, an optimum-off facility should be provided to minimise the heating overrun at the end of the school day.

Careful design of the number and size of boilers to match load variations is required to ensure optimum efficiency throughout the heating season and to have a reasonable standby capacity when implementing major boiler maintenance.

It should be remembered that plant sized for steady-state design conditions always has excess capacity when outside conditions are less severe than design conditions. Plant over-sizing in excess of 25% of steady-state design requirements is unlikely to be justified unless very substantial deviations in flow temperatures are required. Reference should be made to Sections A2, A3, and A9 of the CIBSE Guide when calculating the heat losses and designing the heating system.

Where multiple boiler installations are being designed, condensing boilers should be considered for the lead boilers to take advantage of hot water loads and the long run time for the base load of the space heating.

Small stand-alone gas-fired boilers or direct gas-fired heaters used in remote classrooms can allow more flexible use of the buildings than large central boiler plant.

Heat pumps[4] may be a viable option for the heating in rural schools away from gas main networks. Heat pumps can be air to air, air to water, or water to water. Supplementary heating is normally required when external temperatures fall below around 3°C. This can be by use of a heat store and off-peak electric heating.

References
[4] Department for Education, Broadsheet 22, *Use of Heat Pumps in Rural Schools*, DFE Publications Centre, P.O.Box 2193, London, E15 2EU.

Choice of fuel

The selected fuel should be that giving the lowest net present value taking into account capital, maintenance and running costs. In practice the selection procedure is complicated by the unpredictability of fuel price trends and fuel availability.

Fuel choice in relation to the total carbon dioxide produced is covered in Section F. In the choice of heating systems the option should be kept open where possible to change from one type of fuel to another during the life of a building. Dual fuel burners for oil and gas are readily available and allow the site manager to choose the cheaper fuel. Where oil tanks already exist the extra cost is small.

Electric off-peak storage heater installations cannot be adapted to any other fuel use, whereas systems where heat is delivered by hot water or warm air can possibly be converted to coal, gas, oil or electricity. Electric storage heaters are also unresponsive to changing heat gains.

Heating control

The type of space heating control and the way in which it is operated have a significant influence on fuel consumption. Investing in control equipment can produce a relatively quick pay-back, and zone control of buildings can help with lettings and out of hours use.

Space heating controls should be user-friendly, reliable and as far as possible automatic. Simple and inexpensive controls are now available which provide variable time control with optimum start. These controls are economic even in the smallest of schools. Adjustable components (such as temperature sensors) should be tamper-proof.

Tamper-proof thermostatic radiator valves (TRVs) have been shown to give good local control of heat emitters to minimise overheating and underheating of areas with different thermal mass and incidental heat gains.

It is preferable if a member of the school staff can easily change heating periods, set holidays, change temperatures according to use and extend heating periods.

Good design of heating controls alone is not sufficient to ensure fuel economy. It is also necessary for the controls to be properly commissioned and maintained in good working order. Manuals for the user should be available along with training for the site staff and provision of back-up service advice should it be required.

A user guide should tell school staff how to operate those parts of the heating system over which they can and should exercise control.

Where a building energy management system is provided it can be used to monitor electrical and thermal energy as well as water consumption. It can also help to monitor running costs.

One of the most effective ways of conserving energy in existing schools is to improve the efficiency and responsiveness of the heating installation so that it comes as close as possible to the performance of a well designed new installation. Improvements that may be worthwhile range from the re-design and renewal of plant to the re-assessment of its operating pattern. Fuller details are given in Building Bulletin 73.[5]

Heating zones should be chosen to suit the solar and incidental heat gains and to allow out of hours use of selected zones.

A particular problem is offices which may be the only part of the building occupied during the holidays. Here, electric heating can be used as an alternative to the main heating system.

Control strategies for primary schools

Optimum start/stop controls and automatic frost protection will normally be provided. Zoning and individual temperature sensors should be provided to account for orientation and pattern of use.

Occupancy sensors and manual override to allow occasional use out of hours should also be considered. Weather compensation should be used where the boiler plant capacity exceeds 100 kW and may also be usefully applied to smaller heating zones, eg, to allow for aspect zoning. Weather compensation may be of the central plant or the local zones. It is not advised on circuits serving fan convectors.

Modular boilers (perhaps using a condensing lead boiler) should be considered. Smaller installations can economically use condensing boilers with underfloor heating systems.

Hot water generation should be on a separate circuit or a separate system to the main heating.

Depending on diversity and out of hours use a building energy management system may be considered. This will only be successful where a member of staff is available who is fully conversant with its operation and ensures the system is running correctly.

An economic assessment of cost savings and payback periods should be made before installing complex control systems. The calculations should include maintenance costs of the control equipment and its anticipated life expectancy.

Control strategies for large secondary schools

In addition to the points covered above for primary schools, large secondary schools require careful design of the control system to take account of the greater range of operating hours and diversity of use including possible out of hours use by the local community.

A number of zones may be provided to allow only the areas that are used to be heated. Care should be taken to ensure that the heat load required in these areas can be provided from the heating system efficiently by avoiding long distribution runs and ensuring the boiler plant can operate efficiently at part load.

References
[5] Department for Education, Building Bulletin 73, *A guide to energy efficient refurbishment*, HMSO, 1991, ISBN 0 11 270772 6, £8.50.

References

[1] CIBSE Guide, Section A2, *Weather and Solar Data.*

[2] DfEE Building Bulletin 77, *Designing for pupils with special educational needs: special schools*, HMSO 1992, ISBN 0 11 270796 3, £14.95

[3] Approved Document L (*Conservation of fuel and power*) in support of the Building Regulations, Department of the Environment and Welsh Office, 1994, ISBN 0 11 752933 8, £11.

[4] Department for Education, Broadsheet 22, *Use of Heat Pumps in Rural Schools*, DFE Publications Centre, P.O.Box 2193, London, E15 2EU.

[5] Department for Education, Building Bulletin 73, *A guide to energy efficient refurbishment*, HMSO, 1991, ISBN 0 11 270772 6, £8.50.

BRE Report BR262 *Thermal Insulation: Avoiding risks*, Building Research Establishment, 1994, ISBN 0 11 701792 2, £16.50.

BRE IP 12/94, *Thermal Bridges, Assessing condensation risk and heat losss at thermal bridges around openings*, Building Research Establishment.

BS 6880: 1988 *Code of practice for low temperature hot water heating systems of output greater than 45kW.*

CIBSE Applications Manual AM1:1985, *Automatic controls and their implications for systems design.*

Frost protection

When unoccupied, a building should be heated only for frost protection or during the pre-occupation heat-up period. Frost protection is for the hot and cold water services and the heating system only, unless there is a need to preserve the structure, as with wooden panels in ancient buildings.

A three stage frost protection is recommended for larger heating systems. Designs often omit stage 2 or 3 but the cost saving is small. The set points quoted are for bimetallic thermostats. Electronic temperature sensors have much smaller switching differentials allowing set points to be lower which saves energy.

Stage 1. An outside thermostat located in a position which cannot be affected by sunlight to bring on all pumps both heating and hot water service. This should be set to 2°C (just above freezing).

Stage 2. An immersion/strap-on thermostat should be fitted in the common return from the heating and hot water service which will bring into operation the boiler plant. This should be set at 5°C. Conventional optimisers often provide this function. The water temperature should rise high enough to prevent freezing of remote pipework due to very low outside temperatures and to prevent back-end corrosion of oil boilers. This can be achieved by providing a timer to ensure that the plant runs for 30-60 minutes dependent on the size of the system.

Stage 3. A standard low temperature thermostat installed in a normally heated room with maximum exposure should be set to bring the boiler plant into operation when the internal temperature drops below 5°C. This temperature should be adequate for most buildings where condensation is not a problem.

Where pipework runs externally or the boilerhouse has a poorer level of insulation than the heated spaces, the stage 1 and 2 themostats may need to be set to higher temperatures.

Suitable indicators should be provided to show on the boiler control panel that the various stages of frost protection are working.

An outside air temperature sensor should not be used to directly bring on the boiler plant.

This method of protection assumes that domestic hot water and cold water services are within the insulated building envelope. If they are not, additional frost protection for these services may be needed.

Single stage frost protection, omitting stages 1 and 2 is adequate for smaller gas fired heating systems.

In a building with high thermal storage, the use of night setback operation should be considered for unoccupied hours during term time. This would 'top up' heating as required but rely mainly on stored heat in the fabric to avoid frost damage. This could use less energy than the frost thermostat protection and reduce boost heating requirements on start up for this type of building.

In some highly vulnerable areas, consideration should be given to using self-regulating tracer cable as a last resort. This should be switched on and off by a thermostat set at 2°C.

Where air via fresh air inlets is heated by hot water heater batteries, provision of frost temperature sensors to protect them is essential. When the plant is not operational, the control valve should be open to the coil and the associated dampers closed.

Section D: Ventilation

The School Premises Regulations

(1) All occupied areas in a school building shall have controllable ventilation at a minimum rate of 3 litres of fresh air per second for each of the maximum number of persons the area will accommodate.

(2) All teaching accommodation, medical examination or treatment rooms, sick rooms, isolation rooms, sleeping and living accommodation shall also be capable of being ventilated at a minimum rate of 8 litres of fresh air per second for each of the usual number of people in those areas when such areas are occupied.

(3) All washrooms shall also be capable of being ventilated at a rate of at least six air changes an hour.

(4) Adequate measures shall be taken to prevent condensation in, and remove noxious fumes from, every kitchen and other room in which there may be steam or fumes.

Recommended constructional standards

The heating system shall be capable of maintaining the required room air temperatures with the minimum average background ventilation of 3 litres per second of fresh air per person.

Spaces where noxious fumes or dust are generated may need additional ventilation. Laboratories may require the use of fume cupboards, which should be designed in accordance with DfEE Design Note 29. Design technology areas may require local exhaust ventilation.

All washrooms in which at least 6 air changes per hour cannot be achieved on average by natural means should be mechanically ventilated and the air expelled from the building.

Wherever possible school buildings should be naturally ventilated. However, supplementary mechanical ventilation may be required in spaces with high functional heat gains, eg, kitchens, home economics rooms, and some types of laboratories, and areas producing water vapour or fumes.

Where mechanical ventilation is required heat recovery can reduce heat losses by 50%. However, there will be additional electricity used by the fans; and filters, ductwork and grilles will need maintenance. Ventilation systems must be designed together with any fume cupboards so that they do not disturb the operation of the fume cupboards.[1]

Natural ventilation is driven by the combined wind and stack effect. The rates of natural ventilation required by The School Premises Regulations correspond to the design conditions of average wind speed and average inside to outside temperature difference. In practice, adequate ventilation rates may be higher or lower than the rates quoted. Less ventilation will be required where the use of a space is intermittent, where the volume of a space is large, providing a large dilution effect, or where rapid ventilation occurs between teaching periods, eg, by opening of external windows and doors. As it is difficult to predict the actual rates required, the emphasis should be on the provision of easily adjustable openings whether they are windows, slot ventilators or air grilles.

The ventilation system should be designed to ensure that air movement at the occupants' level is at such a temperature and velocity as to ensure comfort; window design is important for this. Background ventilation is required whenever spaces are occupied. Trickle vents controlled by the occupants are an effective way of providing this by natural ventilation.

References
[1] DfEE, Design Note 29, *Fume Cupboards,* (to be revised).

Section D: Ventilation

References

[1] DfEE, Design Note 29, *Fume Cupboards,* (to be revised).

[2] Department for Education Building Bulletin 79, *Passive solar schools, a design guide,* 1994, ISBN 0 11 270876 5, £19.95.

[3] Approved Document F *(Ventilation)* in support of the Building Regulations, Department of the Environment and Welsh Office, 1994, ISBN 0 11 752932 X, £4.50

[4] Approved Document L *(Conservation of fuel and power)* in support of the Building Regulations, Department of the Environment and Welsh Office, 1994, ISBN 0 11 752933 8, £11.

BRE Digest 399, *Natural Ventilation in non-domestic buildings,* 1994, ISBN 0 85125 645 7.

CIBSE Applications Manual AM10: *Natural Ventilation in Non-Domestic Buildings,* 1997, ISBN 0 900953 77 2, £45.

Where appropriate, consideration should be given to the design of the building so that natural ventilation can be driven by the solar induced stack effect. This will encourage ventilation on days with little or no wind.

Measures to limit solar gain should be considered as part of the ventilation design. The ventilation rates for cooling in summer need to be excessively high if no measures are taken to prevent solar gains.[2]

Natural ventilation designs for background and rapid ventilation using the openable areas quoted in Table 2 of Part F of the Building Regulations[3] should satisfy the requirements for ventilation except in the case of deep plan spaces where more complex design methods are required to predict the natural ventilation rates.

The methods range from manual calculations of air flow through windows or across a space to simple single zone computer models through multi-zone models to computerised fluid dynamic models. An alternative which has also been used to good effect is to use scale models with salt solutions to model the air flows.

In a well insulated building, ventilation heat losses account for a major part of the energy consumed. Infiltration through joints in the external envelope, around door and window openings and service penetrations can represent a large part of these losses and should be reduced as far as possible.[4] Draught lobbies, auto-closing doors and internal fire doors can all play their part in reducing infiltration.

The design should ensure ease of maintenance. This includes the replacement of filters, the cleaning of extract grilles and the cleaning of ventilation ductwork.

Section E: Hot and cold water supplies

The School Premises Regulations

Water Supplies

(1) A school shall have a wholesome supply of water for domestic purposes including a supply of drinking water.

(2) Water closets and urinals shall have an adequate supply of cold water and washbasins, sinks, baths and showers shall have an adequate supply of hot and cold water.

(3) The temperature of hot water supplies to baths and showers shall not exceed 43°C.

Drainage

(1) A school shall be provided with an adequate drainage system for hygienic purposes and the general disposal of waste water and surface water.

Recommended constructional standards

Cold water storage capacity in day schools should not exceed 25 litres per occupant.

All water fittings should be of a type approved by the WRC (Water Research Centre), and all installations should comply with the Water Supplies Byelaws.[1]

Where a temperature regime is used to reduce the risk of *legionellosis* hot water storage temperatures should not be lower than 60°C. However for occupant safety, to reduce the risk of scalding, The School Premises Regulations require that the temperature at point of use should not be above 43°C for baths and showers and where occupants are severely disabled. This may be achieved by thermostatic mixing at the point of use. It is also recommended that hot water supplies to washbasins in nursery and primary schools are limited to 43°C. Particular attention should be given to the provision of facilities to ensure the effective maintenance of systems.[2,3]

Unvented hot water storage systems should comply with Building Regulations, Part G3, 1992.

Cold water

Tanks should be as small as possible commensurate with the requirements of the local water supply company. In day schools it should not be neccessary to exceed 25 litres per occupant. The minimum recommended[4,5] storage capacities per pupil for different types of school are shown below. The figures allow for 24 hour storage. Some water supply companies do not require this and the figures can then be reduced.

The size of water meter should also be as small as possible, as standing charges increase with the meter size.

An adequate supply of drinking water should be accessible to staff and pupils throughout the school day.[6]

Table 3

Day schools	
Nursery and primary	15 litres per pupil
Secondary	20 litres per pupil
Boarding school	90 litres per pupil

Hot water

The use of a decentralized hot water system may help to minimise energy wastage. Wherever possible a separate boiler, hot water generator or point of use water heater should be used to provide hot water. Plant sizing curves for hot water in schools are given in Section B4 of the CIBSE Guide.[5]

Numbers of sanitary appliances for different types of schools are given in The School Premises Regulations, 1996.

Legionellosis (including legionnaires' disease)

Inhalation of the *legionella* bacteria can give rise to *legionellosis*, but the risk of infection is low. Aerosols produced by water services such as showers and spray taps are potential routes of infection.

Although there have been no known cases of legionnaires' disease in schools this is no reason for complacency. Schools need to be aware of the dangers and their responsibility to maintain water systems properly.

In accordance with the HSC Approved Code of Practice *The prevention or control of legionellosis*[7], risk assessments are required for certain water systems. Where a reasonable foreseeable risk is assessed, management plans should be drawn up and maintained to minimise the risk by regular inspection, maintenance, cleaning and treatment procedures.

Whilst surveys have shown *legionella* to be present in quite large numbers of water systems such as those found in hospitals, schools and office blocks, only rarely do these appear to give rise to infection. It is generally not possible to completely and permanently eradicate the bacteria. Therefore, in practice, the risk of infection is addressed by the application of good engineering practice to ensure the bacteria are prevented from proliferating. A considerable amount of guidance has been issued on the risks. Compliance with HS(G)70 *The control of legionellosis*[8] and HSC Approved Code of Practice *The prevention or control of legionellosis* is a minimum requirement. Good practical guidance on procedures is also available.[2&3]

Steps should be taken to minimise the opportunity for growth of *legionella*. It multiplies in warm water (approximately 20 to 45°C) and will thrive in the presence of biofilms, scale or debris. The temperature at cold water outlets should be not more than 3°C higher than the cold water storage temperature, which can be as high as 25°C, the highest temperature at which the Water Companies can supply water. Consequently quick water turnover in storage tanks is crucial in preventing the proliferation of legionella.

Where a temperature regime is relied upon to control *legionella* hot water should be stored at a temperature of 60°C or above and distributed at a minimum temperature of 50°C.

However for occupant safety, to reduce the risk of scalding, The School Premises Regulations require that the temperature at point of use should not be above 43°C for baths and showers and where occupants are severely disabled. This may be achieved by thermostatic mixing at the point of use. It is also recommended that hot water supplies to washbasins in nursery and primary schools are limited to 43°C.

Because the organism thrives in warm (but not hot) water, the length of piping carrying hot and cold water (eg, after a thermostatic mixer valve) must be kept to an absolute minimum, certainly less than 2 metres. Preferably each shower head should have its own mixer valve. Similarly, the length of pipes feeding washbasin hot taps should be minimised, especially with spray head taps which could generate an aerosol containing *legionella*; point of use water heaters may be preferable to centralised hot water systems.

Recent research on silver/copper ionisation water treatment has shown that this can be a successful alternative to a temperature regime, to control *legionellosis*[9]. The research has also established that copper pipework is naturally biocidal particularly at slightly acid pH values. Copper can inhibit the formation of biofilms which are the breeding ground for *legionella* and other bacteria. Copper pipework must have water passing through it in the first few months for the natural inhibition to take place. It should not be left empty for long periods. As a result of this research the HSE are issuing a supplement to HS(G)70.[8]

Past outbreaks of legionnaires' disease have usually been associated with systems that have been neglected, or where the routine operation has changed. Frequent monitoring of the operation of the system and factors encouraging rapid multiplication of bacteria are therefore vital control measures.

Excessive periods of stagnation (in tanks or 'dead legs') should be avoided, and storage tanks must be maintained in a clean condition. Water tanks should comply with the Water Supplies Byelaws.[1]

GRP tanks usually contain biofilms therefore annual chlorination followed by cleaning is recommended. Chlorination of copper pipework should be avoided as it strips off the natural protection of the pipe and can cause corrosion. Chlorination of hot and cold water services should be done in accordance with HS(G)70 recommended concentrations and chlorination times.

As sampling for *legionella* will often yield positive results, it is not advocated as a routine measure because it can cause either unnecessary alarm and anxiety to all concerned, or complacency and relaxation of standards. Sampling is expensive, and since no firm conclusions can be drawn from the results, the random sampling for *legionella* does not represent good value for money.

On the other hand, monitoring general water quality can provide a fair indication of system conditions. This, together with a package of other routine measures recommended by HSE, will draw attention to potential problems as they develop.

References

[1] Water Research Council, *Water Supplies Byelaws Guide*, 2nd edition, 1989, £7.95, ISBN 0 90215671 3. (Note: the Byelaws are to be replaced by the Water Regulations.)

See also the Water Research Council publication, *The Water Fittings and Materials Directory*.

[2] Chartered Institution of Building Services Engineers (CIBSE), Technical Memorandum 13, 1991, *Minimising the risk of Legionnaires disease*, ISBN 0 900953 52 7.

[3] *Guide to Legionellosis, Temperature measurements for hot and cold water services*, BSRIA Application Guide AG4/94, N.L. Pavey, ISBN 0 86022 3.

[4] BS 6700: 1987, British Standard Specification for *Design, installation, testing and maintenance of services supplying water for domestic use within buildings and their curtillages*, ISBN 0 580 15769 5.

[5] CIBSE Guide, Section B4: *Water Service Systems*, 1986, ISBN 0 9009533 30 6.

[6] *Workplace (Health, Safety and Welfare) Regulations 1992, Guidance for the Education Sector*, Leaflet IAC(L)97, HSE Books.

[7] Health and Safety Executive, HSC Approved code of practice, L8, *The prevention or control of Legionellosis including Legionnaires' disease*, 1995.

[8] Health and Safety Executive, HS(G)70, *The control of legionellosis including Legionnaires' disease*, 1994 (supplement to be issued), ISBN 0 1 882150 4.

[9] *Ionisation water treatment for hot and cold water services*, BSRIA Technical Note TN 6/96, N.L.Pavey, ISBN 0 86022 438 4.

Legionella and Building Services, G.W.Brundrett, Buttersworth Heinemann, ISBN 0 7506 1528 1.

Section F: Energy (carbon dioxide) rating

General

In the sections dealing with environmental conditions a number of measures for conserving energy have been recommended.

There are a variety of calculation methods available to predict the annual energy consumption and the amount of CO_2 produced by new buildings.

The most sophisticated are computerised real time models which use recorded weather data to simulate the actual performance of the building. These models require the input of a lot of parameters and are most useful at the later stages of design when the form of the building is known in some detail.

At the early stage of design when assessing different options a steady state calculation method can be more useful.

Such a method follows. It allows alternative designs to be ranked in terms of their cost-effectiveness and their environmental impact in terms of CO_2 production. It provides a procedure for comparison of alternative methods of heating and lighting. Calculated energy consumptions in kWh per square metre floor area are converted into $kgCO_2/m^2$ using the conversion factors of the various fuels.

Design procedure

The calculation procedure enables the energy requirements to be estimated at an early stage in the design.

Kitchens and swimming pools are not included and their areas and energy consumptions must be excluded from the calculations. Craftwork and home economics loads are also not included.

The calculation procedure derives an Annual CO_2 Production Value by the summation of the heat requirement of the building and the energy used for other purposes such as lighting, small power, hot water, and the circulating pumps for the heating system. The heat requirement is calculated from the theoretical heat loss minus the heat displaced by adventitious gains such as lighting, occupancy, small power use, and solar gains. Using this basis the annual energy uses are calculated over a model year and converted to $kgCO_2/m^2$.

The total Annual CO_2 Production Value is calculated and compared with the target bands in Figures 1 and 2 for primary and secondary schools respectively. The figures show bands of annual energy consumption in terms of $kgCO_2$ per square metre of the gross floor area (GFA) that is heated.

As the design of the building develops, alternatives (eg, in the choice of fuel, fuel efficiency or the methods of heating and lighting) may present themselves.

Realistic estimates of the options and the consequent life cycle costs for operation and maintenance are required so that design decisions can be based on both cost and environmental impact.

A spreadsheet calculation for an example school is given on pages 32-35. A blank spreadsheet and a spreadsheet formula sheet are included on pages 37 and 38.

The Annual CO_2 production value target bands were first published in the Schools' Environmental Assessment Method (SEAM), Building Bulletin 83 in October 1996. These target bands have now been revised in the light of a survey of 1995/96 energy consumption in 2000 primary schools and 300 secondary schools from 17 local authorities.

Bands E and F (shown dotted) now apply only to existing schools. Previously only band F applied to existing buildings and not to new buildings. The revised target bands and numbers of points awarded should now be used in the SEAM assessment.

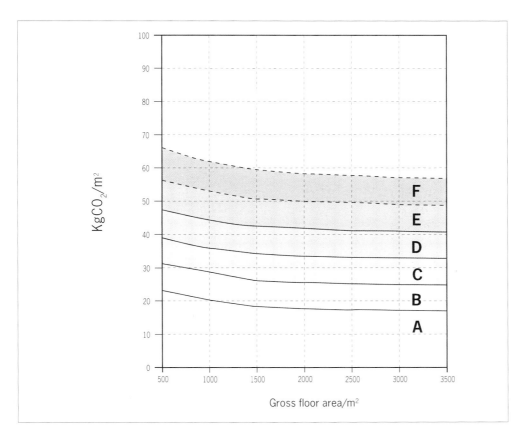

Figure 1:
Annual CO_2 production value targets: primary schools

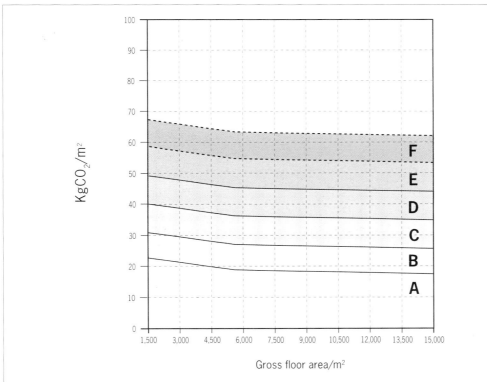

Figure 2:
Annual CO_2 production value targets: secondary schools

Key to figures 1 and 2

BAND	COMMENT
D	Upper line of band indicates the maximum permissible Annual CO_2 Production Value for **new** buildings.
C and **B**	Improvement upon the maximum permissible Annual CO_2 Production Value.
A	Good low energy design.

Band	A	B	C	D	E	F
New buildings	7	5	3	1		
Existing buildings	11	9	7	5	3	1

Table 4:
The table shows the revised numbers of points to be awarded in the SEAM method, bands E and F now only apply to existing buildings

Table 5:
Degree-days.

Degree-days are a measure of how cold the weather is during the heating season (1st September to 30th April for schools).

The number of degree-days equals the sum of the number of days times the number of degrees that the temperature is less than the base temperature.

The table gives 20 year average degree-days (for 1975 to 1995) to a base of 15.5°C for each of the recognised zones within England and Wales.

Degree-days are usually quoted to a base temperature of 15.5°C. This is lower than room temperature and allows for occupancy and miscellaneous gains. However this calculation method does not apply this correction and uses a base temperature equal to the room temperature of 18°C for classrooms. Note: current annual and 20 year degree-day figures should be used if available.

Location	Zone	Degree-days
Thames Valley	1	1678
South East	2	1838
Southern	3	1792
South West	4	1512
Severn Valley	5	1588
Midlands	6	2014
West Pennines	7	1980
North West	8	2040
Borders	9	2110
North East	10	1977
East Pennines	11	1938
East Anglia	12	1897
Wales	16	1732
Average		**1856**

Model Year - Hours of operation[1] of space heating

It is necessary to construct a model year on which to base calculations so that comparisons can be made. For this purpose a normal school day is used. Evening and holiday use is excluded as this varies from school to school. Likewise, kitchens, swimming pools and other process loads are excluded from the calculations. The length of heating season, 1st September - 30th April, is 176 working days. The number of school days, including 8 days for cleaning and maintenance is 144.

The average value of degree-days, D_d for England and Wales over the school heating season for normal working hours is 1856 (use local figure for D_d from Table 5).

Assuming a medium weight building (as most school buildings are) and intermittent use of plant and disregarding occupancy and other miscellaneous gains, the base temperature equals the internal design temperature (Section C recommends 18°C for classrooms).

In order to correct the degree days for other base temperatures, the figure for base temperature of 15.5°C should be adjusted by the relevant factor in Table B18.9 of CIBSE Guide Section B18[1]:

Base temperature $= 18°C$

ratio $D_d/D_{15.5} = 1.30$

The following equivalent hours calculation is based on the CIBSE Guide.[1] Box 1 explains this calculation and the correction factors which must be applied for mode of operation.

Average equivalent annual operation:

$$E = \frac{24 \times D_{15.5} \times 1.30}{19}$$

Correction for mode of operation

(a) 5 day week (for school use)
$$W \times DR = 0.8 \times (144/176)$$
$$= 0.65$$

(b) intermittent use...$R_p = 0.70$

(c) 7.5 hour day.......$D_l = 0.96$

Corrected $E_c = 24 \times D_{15.5} \times 1.30/19$
$\times 0.65 \times 0.70 \times 0.96$

Box 1: Corrected equivalent hours of operation

The method uses local degree-days and the design temperature to represent the space heating requirement in terms of the equivalent number of hours at full load operation.

$$E = \frac{24 \times D_d}{\Delta t_d}$$

Where:

$E =$ Equivalent hours of operation at full load.

$D_d =$ Seasonal total of degree days to the base of the design internal temperature.

$\Delta t_d =$ Design internal temperature minus design external temperature.

Correction for mode of operation

The calculated equivalent hours is adjusted by a series of correction factors (detailed below) appertaining to the building's mode of operation, which produces a corrected equivalent hours of operation. This value is used to determine the heating requirement of the building.

$E_c = E \times W \times DR \times R_p \times D_l$

$E_c =$ Corrected equivalent hours of operation at full load.

$W =$ Factor for length of working week.

$DR =$ Ratio of school operating days to office operating days.

$R_p =$ Factor for the response of the building and plant.

$D_l =$ Factor for the length of the school day.

References
[1] CIBSE Guide B18 - *Installation and Equipment Data*, 1988.

a. Length of working week (W)

Schools are most commonly medium weight buildings when a factor of 0.8 is used for a 5 day working week.

The values of W in Table 6 were designed for office buildings which have 176 working days during the defined heating season (September to April inclusive).

Ratio of school to office operating days (DR)

Schools operate for fewer days than offices over the same heating season and total school operating days, including 8 days for cleaning, are generally 144. Therefore a further correction has to be applied to make the factor W suitable for school buildings.

The factor DR is obtained by a ratio of the number of operating days.

For school use: the additional factor, DR is generally: (144/176) = 0.82.

b. Response of building and plant (R_p).

Most schools are intermittently heated, although the heating may be responsive or have a long time lag and consideration should be given to the type of system when using these correction factors. See Table 7.

c. Length of working day (D_l)

Educational buildings commonly have a daily occupancy of 7.5 hours. See Table 8.

Recommended design data

The values in the boxes that follow are recommended in the absence of more accurate information. More accurate figures, eg, lighting gains based on the actual lighting design, should be used when they become available.

In the tables that follow the buildings are categorised into light, medium, and heavy weight buildings, this refers to their thermal capacity which may include considerations for the buildings' contents as well as their construction.

Definition of light, medium and heavy, weight buildings.

Heavy weight:

buildings of curtain walling, masonry or concrete, especially multi-storey, with solid internal walls, eg, inner city, particularly Victorian, two and three storey buildings.

Medium weight:

traditional brick-built, single-storey or concrete multi-storey with large windows.

Light weight:

system or temporary buildings with light weight partitions and external walls.

Working week	Type of construction		
	Light weight	Medium weight	Heavy weight
7 day	1.0	1.0	1.0
5 day	0.75	0.80	0.85

Table 6:
Factor W for length of working week.

Type of heating	Type of construction		
	Light weight	Medium weight	Heavy weight
Intermittent-responsive plant	0.55	0.70	0.85
Intermittent-plant with long lag	0.55	0.70	0.85
Continuous	1.0	1.0	1.0

Table 7:
Factor R_p for response of building and plant.

Occupied period (hours)	Type of construction		
	Light weight	Medium weight	Heavy weight
4	0.68	0.82	0.96
7.5	0.96	0.98	0.99
8	1.0	1.0	1.0
12	1.25	1.14	1.03

Table 8:
Factor D_l for length of working day.

Section F: Energy (carbon dioxide) rating

Table 9:
Building fabric U-values

Opaque areas	Watts/m²/°C
Walls	0.4
Floor	0.4
Roof	0.3
Roof with a loft	0.25
U-values for windows	
Single glazed (timber)	4.7
Double glazed (timber)	2.8
Rooflights	2.8

Occupancy gains

For this calculation procedure, a constant rate of heat production from the occupants is used. The total heat produced is estimated from the number of occupants within the building.

Typical rate of heat production
70 watts per pupil

Figure 3

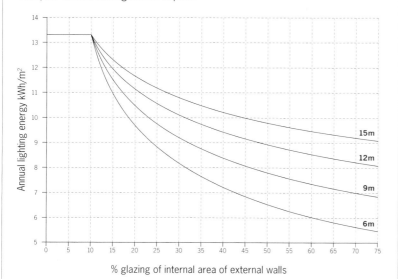

Annual lighting energy consumption in relation to vertical glazed area of external walls, for various average room depths.

y-axis: Annual lighting energy kWh/m²
x-axis: % glazing of internal area of external walls

(curves labelled 15m, 12m, 9m, 6m)

The graph above is based upon the following assumptions:

- Lights are switched on and off in response to daylight levels;
- electric lighting is needed for the number of hours that the daylight is below 300 Lux as given in the table below for different design daylight factors;

Daylight Factor (DF)	Number of hours when daylight is below 300 Lux
DF below 0.5	1640 hours
DF 0.5 to 1.0	1600 hours
DF 1.0 to 2.0	1280 hours
DF 2.0 to 4.0	700 hours
DF over 4.0	250 hours

- a minimum maintained illuminance for general teaching spaces of 300 Lux, which can be provided at a loading of 8 W/m²;
- reflection factors: walls - 30% (average including pinboard areas), ceiling - 70%, floor - 15%; and
- floor-ceiling height 2.4m, window height 1.5m, cill height 0.9m.

If rooflights are used, their glazed area is multiplied by 180 degrees minus the angle of the rooflight to the horizontal, divided by 90 degrees, eg, 1m² horizontal rooflight is equivalent to 2m² of vertical window. This equivalent area is then added to the area of the vertical glazing to determine the percentage glazing of the internal face of the external walls.

Electric lighting

The average room depth should be calculated. For example, a daylit building would have an average room depth of from 6 - 9m. The average room depths and percentages of glazing on the internal areas of the external walls are used to find the lighting energy in kWh/m² using Figure 3 on the left.

The prediction of annual lighting energy use obtained from Figure 3 is based on a design load of 8 W/m² and a design minimum maintained illuminance of 300 lux at desk height. More accurate information for the proposed design may be used if available.

Typical load
8 watts/m² for an illuminance of 300 Lux

Ventilation losses

The background ventilation (infiltration) rate will depend upon the type of window system used and the air leakage characteristics of the building construction.

If a heat recovery system is used, the ventilation losses can be reduced by 50%. However, there will be additional electrical energy used for fan power and a need for maintenance of filters, ductwork and grilles.

Minimum ventilation requirement
3 litres/second/person of fresh air

Typical ventilation rate
4 – 6 litres/second/person of fresh air

Hot water service

Hot water energy use varies according to the type and use of the building. However as an approximation the figure below may be used.

Typical rate	2 watts/m²
This value does not include hot water use for kitchens	

Heating circulators

Fans and pumps for use in the heating system are often located outside of the building in which case they will produce an electrical load but no heat gain.

Typical load	2 watts/m²

Miscellaneous power gains

Included in the figure below, are all small power teaching uses such as computers and audio-visual equipment. It is also intended to include the use of general cleaning equipment.

Individual high load equipment such as kilns and cooking appliances are not included in the calculation.

Teaching and cleaning equipment	5 watts/m²

Solar Gains

Most buildings benefit from solar heat gains to some extent. If careful consideration is given to the use of solar gains at the design stage these benefits can be optimised[2] (see Section C).

Design and methods of using solar gains are many and varied and separate independent calculations or computer simulations can be used to assess the effects of different designs. However, a simple method of accounting for the effect of direct solar gains on space heating is included in this calculation procedure. The solar gains are calculated using a solar utilitization factor related to the area of glazing, the orientation of the window and the type of glazing used

(ie, single, double or triple). This method is based on Section B5.2 of the CIBSE Applications Manual on Window Design[3].

The solar gains are calculated from the formula:

$$\text{Solar gain} = \sum ([\text{areas} \times \text{solar utilization}] \times \Delta t_d \times E_c) / (\text{gross floor area} \times 1000)$$

Where solar utilisation[3] $= \dfrac{1000 f T_s TS}{0.24 D_d}$

and:

$f = 0.65$

$T = 0.87 \text{(single) or } 0.76 \text{ (double) or } 0.66 \text{ (triple glazing)}[3]$

$T_s = 0.8$

The average solar radiation on a vertical surface

$S = 1.5$ (north),

4.31 (south),

2.43 (east & west),

3.96 (horizontal)

$D_d = 1.3 \times D_{15.5}$

The equation reduces to:

$$\text{Solar gain} = \sum (\text{areas} \times S \times 100 \times f \times T_s \times T \times W \times DR \times R_p \times D_l) / (\text{gross floor area})$$

Values for S, f, T_s and T are taken from Section B5 of the CIBSE Applications Manual which describes the calculation method in more depth and gives tables for these factors.

W, DR, R_p and D_l are from the CIBSE determination of the Model Year described on pages 28 and 29.

(See example calculation on page 33, paragraph f. Solar gains).

Other gains and energy uses

The period of full occupancy at 5 hours per day is taken for metabolic gains during the heating season, (ie, $136 \times 5 = 680$ hours). [5 hours is used in preference to 7.5 hours to allow for lunch and other breaks and for class changeover]

References
[2] Department for Education, Building Bulletin 79, *Passive Solar Schools, a design guide*, HMSO 1994, ISBN 0 11 270876 5, £19.95.

[3] CIBSE Applications Manual *Window Design AM2: Section B5.2 Useful Heat Gains* 1987, ISBN 0 900953 33 0.

Hot water and miscellaneous power requirements are assumed for 1500 hours per annum = (7.5hrs x 200days); useful heat gains from them are provided only over the heating season for 1020 hours = (7.5hrs x 136days). [136 days is the fully occupied part of the heating season, ie, minus the 8 cleaning days]

Heating circulators and fans operate over the heating season only, for 1080 hours per annum = (7.5hrs x 144 days).

It is assumed that 80% of the lighting is used over the heating season and that this contributes useful heat to the space.

Table 10

Type of system	Seasonal efficiency %		
Space heating:			
Electric			
Fan assisted electric off-peak heaters	90		
Direct electric floor and ceiling systems	95		
Gas/Oil boiler type	Conventional	High performance	Condensing
Automatic centrally fired radiator or convector system	63	76	87
Automatic centrally fired warm air ventilation system	60	73	84
Domestic hot water heating:			
Gas and oil fired boiler/storage cylinder	56		
Off-peak electric storage with cylinder & immersion heater	80		
Instantaneous gas multi-point heater	62		
Instantaneous electric multi-point heater	95		
District heating with central calorifiers and distribution	56		

Table 11

KgCO$_2$ per kWh of delivered energy	
Electricity	0.58
Natural gas	0.21
Solid fuel	0.34
Oil	0.29
Sustainable wood or biomass fuel	0.01

In the case of systems using heat pumps, the CO$_2$ conversion factors for whichever fuel is used by the heat pump, should be divided by the coefficient of performance of the heat pump.

Kilogrammes of carbon dioxide can be converted to tonnes of carbon by multiplying by 0.048

Seasonal system efficiencies averaged over the heating season[1&4] (based on gross calorific values of fuels)

The design heating requirement is divided by the seasonal efficiency of the heating system to obtain the delivered fuel equivalent, ie, the amount of gas, oil or electricity supplied to the school. See Table 10.

Carbon dioxide (CO$_2$) emissions

The level of CO$_2$ produced by different fuels varies according to the initial proportion of carbon and the degree of processing required to arrive at the delivered fuel.

The delivered energy of a fuel is multiplied by the carbon dioxide conversion factor to give the carbon dioxide equivalent. Factors for typical fuels are given in Table 11.

Note that each unit of electricity delivered consumes three times as much primary energy and emits three times as much CO$_2$ as a similar unit of gas due to conversion losses at the power station

Example calculation

To calculate the annual CO$_2$ Production Value for a 450 place, single storey secondary school building with a gross floor area of 3565m^2 and a perimeter of 432m.

Assume a gas-fired central boiler with radiators and hot water storage cylinder, Temperature difference $\Delta t_d = 19°C$ (internal 18°C, external -1°C).

Given:

Local 20 year average for the Midlands
$D_d = 2014$.

Floor-ceiling height	= 2.4m
Overall height	= 3.0m
Room depth (Figure 3)	= 8.0m
Overall window : wall ratio	= 0.29

(internal elevation of external wall)

The building is medium weight. The overall percentage glazing is distributed as follows :

- North   25%
- South   45%
- East   25%
- West   25%

Heating is intermittent with responsive plant, $R_p = 0.70$.

U-values and installed loads are as recommended earlier in this section.

Double glazing and a ventilation rate of $15m^3$/person/hour (4.2 litres/second/person) have been used.

In the example calculation that follows the default values, as in the recommended design data on pages 29 to 32, for U-values (maximum values), incidental gains, domestic hot water loads, lighting loads, miscellaneous power and heating circulator loads have been used.

In practice these values can be considerably improved on and default values should be replaced by actual values where available.

a. Fabric losses

Fabric losses = $\dfrac{\sum(\text{Area} \times \text{U-value}) \times \Delta t_d}{\text{gross floor area}}$

- *example:*
  wall losses = $[(735 \times 0.4) \times 19]/3565$
  $= 1.57 \text{ W/m}^2$

b. Ventilation losses

Ventilation losses
$= \dfrac{[\text{m}^3/\text{person/hour} \times 0.33 \times \Delta t_d]}{(\text{density of occupation})}$

- *example:*
  ventilation losses = $[15 \times 0.33 \times 19]/$
  $(3565/450) = 11.87 \text{ W/m}^2$

c. Miscellaneous power gain

Miscellaneous power
$= [\text{installed load (W/m}^2)] \times [\text{hours of operation}]/1000$

- *example:*
  miscellaneous power = $(5 \times 1020/1000)$
  $= 5.1 \text{ kWh/m}^2$

d. Lighting gain

The value for electric lighting is taken from Figure 3, using the overall glazing ratio and the average room depth. Of this lighting use, 80% is assumed to be during the heating season. This is a useful space heating gain and is used to off-set the heating requirement.

- *example:*
  lighting gain = $0.8 \times 8 = 7.04 \text{ kWh/m}^2$

e. Occupancy gain

Occupancy gain
$= [\text{metabolic rate (W/m}^2) \times \text{number of occupants} \times \text{hours occupied}]/(\text{floor area} \times 1000)$

- *example:*
  occupancy gains $= [70 \times 450 \times 680]/$
  $(3565 \times 1000) = 6.01 \text{ kWh/m}^2$

f. Solar gains

Solar gain $= \sum[(\text{areas} \times S) \times 100 \times f \times T_s \times T \times W \times DR \times R_p \times D_l] / (\text{gross floor area})$

Values for f, T_s and T are from page 31. T = 0.76 for double glazing. W, DR, D_l are from page 29.

- *example:*
  $R_p = 0.70$ from above
  solar gain
  $= [(65 \times 1.5) + (104 \times 4.31) + (65 \times 2.43) +$
  $(65 \times 2.43)] \times (100 \times 0.65 \times 0.8 \times$
  $0.76 \times 144/176 \times 0.7 \times 0.96)/3565$
  $= 4.20 \text{ kWh/m}^2$

The spreadsheet on page 34 shows that for the example school, the predicted annual Carbon Dioxide Production Value is 19.51 $kgCO_2/m^2$ of gross floor area. This has been plotted in Figure 4 on page 35 on the target graph for new secondary schools. The result is just inside band A for good low energy design.

References
[1] CIBSE Guide B18 - *Installation and Equipment Data*, 1988.

[4] Good Practice Guide 16 - Guide for Installers of Condensing Boilers in Commercial Buildings - Energy Efficiency Office Best Practice Programme, October 1990.

Section F: Energy (carbon dioxide) rating

Energy (carbon dioxide) rating calculation sheet
Example Calculation

Floor area	3565		square metres excluding kitchens and swimming pools

Factors for use with Figure 3 in lighting calculation

Average room depth	8	metres
Window : wall ratio	0·29	percentage glazing on internal elevation of external wall

Occupancy	450	persons
Density of occupancy	7·92	square metres of gross floor area per person

Design temperature	Internal	18	°C		
	External	–1	°C	Local 20-year degree day average	2014
	Temperature difference	19	°C		

Model year factors page 28   W 0.8   School days in heating season 144   DR 0.82 R_p 0.70 D_l 0.96

Losses

		Area	U-value	Watts/m²
Opaque area page 33(a)	Walls	735	0·4	1·57
	Roof	3565	0·3	5·70
	Floor	3565	0·4	7·60
Windows	North	65	2·8	0.94
	South	104	2·8	1.50
	East	65	2·8	0.94
	West	65	2·8	0.94
	Rooflights			

Ventilation rate	15 m³/hour/person		Ventilation loss page 33(b) 11·87	Watts/m²

Convert to kWh/m²: (divide by 1000 and multiply by corrected equivalent hours of operation 1455)   **4539**   kWh/m²

Gains

Incidental

	Installed load (W/m²)	Hours of operation	kWh/m²
Miscellaneous power page 33(c)	5	1020	**5·10**
Lighting from Figure 3 page 33(d)			**7·04**

	Metabolic rate (W/person)	Hours of occupancy	
Occupancy page 33(e)	70	680	6.01

Factors for solar gain calculation page 31

Transmission of glazing T 0.76   Utility factor f 0.65   Shadow factor T_s 0.8

Solar gain factor 0.0048

Solar gain pages 31 and 33(f)	Area	Average solar radiation	Solar gain	kWh/m²
North	65	1·5	0·48	
South	104	4.31	2·19	
East	65	2.43	0.77	
West	65	2.43	0.77	
Rooflights	0	3.96	0·00	
Sum of solar gains			**4.20**	

Total gains	**22.35**	kWh/m²
Heating requirement: losses – gains	**23.04**	kWh/m²
Delivered fuel equivalent: (divide by heating system efficiency 0·63)	**35.57**	kWh/m²
Carbon dioxide equivalent: (multiply by carbon dioxide conversion factor 0·21)	**7.68**	KgCO₂/m² **(i)**

Other uses	Installed Load (W/m²)	Hours of operation	kWh/m²
Domestic hot water	2	1500	**3**
Delivered fuel equivalent: (divide by hot water system efficiency 0·56)			**5·36**
Carbon dioxide equivalent: (multiply by carbon dioxide conversion factor 0·21)			**1·13** KgCO₂/m² **(ii)**

Electrical energy	Installed Load (W/m²)	Hours of operation	kWh/m²
Lighting (Figure 3)			**8·8**
Miscellaneous power	5	1500	**7·5**
Heating circulators	2	1080	**2·16**
Total electric			**18·46** kWh/m²
Carbon dioxide equivalent: (multiply by carbon dioxide conversion factor 0·58)			**10·71** KgCO₂/m² **(iii)**

Total Annual Carbon Dioxide Production Value
(heating + hot water + electrical) (i + ii + iii)   **19.51**   **Kg carbon dioxide per square metre of gross floor area**

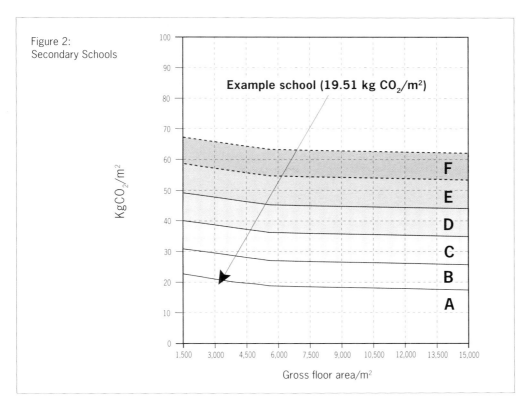

Figure 2:
Secondary Schools

Example school (19.51 kg CO₂/m²)

Figure 4:
The predicted annual CO_2 Production Value, at 19.51 $kgCO_2/m^2$ gross floor area, is in band A considerably better than the maximum permitted Design Target.

References
[1] CIBSE Guide B18 - *Installation and Equipment Data*, 1988.

[2] Department for Education, Building Bulletin 79, *Passive Solar Schools, a design guide*, HMSO 1994, ISBN 0 11 270876 5, £19.95.

[3] CIBSE Applications Manual *Window Design AM2: Section B5.2 Useful Heat Gains* 1987, ISBN 0 900953 33 0.

[4] Good Practice Guide 16 - Guide for Installers of Condensing Boilers in Commercial Buildings - Energy Efficiency Office Best Practice Programme, October 1990.

Department of Trade and Industry, *Digest of UK Energy Statistics*.

Energy Efficiency Best Practice Publications:

Introduction to Energy Efficiency in Sports and Recreation Centres.

Good Practice Guide 129 - *Good housekeeping in dry sports centres.*

Good Practice Guide 130 - *Good housekeeping in swimming pools - a guide for centre managers.*

Good Practice Guide 173 - *Energy efficient design of new buildings and extensions - for schools and colleges*, 1997.

For further information contact BRECSU, address given on page 36.

However there is still scope for improving the energy efficiency of the design.

If the predicted annual CO_2 Production Value had been above the maximum permitted(ie, the top of band D), then the design would have been reconsidered in order to identify the factors which produced the excess energy consumption. These factors would then be altered to improve the design so that it met the design target.

The calculation was repeated with the following energy saving features:

improved U-values of

    roof   = 0.25 W/m²/°C,

    walls and floor = 0.35 W/m²/°C,

    triple glazed timber framed windows
                = 0.8 W/m²/°C;

Total solar radiant heat transmission of triple glazing, T = 0.66

a condensing boiler;

a direct gas-fired hot water generator;

the minimum ventilation rate of 10m³/person/hour;

photoelectric lighting controls; and

a reduced miscellaneous power demand of 3W/m².

The resulting annual CO_2 Production Value was 12.92 $KgCO_2/m^2$, an improvement of 34% on the previous calculation putting the design well inside band A.

This example shows the value of this calculation in early design decisions and that highly energy efficient designs are possible using current construction techniques.

References
Department for Education,
Building Bulletin 73, *A guide to
energy efficient refurbishment*,
ISBN 0 11 270772 6, HMSO,
1991, £8.50.

BRECSU, Department of the
Environment, *Introduction to
Energy Efficiency, Building
Energy Efficiency in Schools, A
guide to a whole school
approach*, 1996.

Reference should also be
made to the Energy Efficiency
Office Good Practice Guides
and Energy Consumption
Guides. These can be obtained
free of charge from the
Building Research
Establishment Conservation
Support Unit (BRECSU),
Building Research
Establishment, Garston,
Watford, WD2 7JR,
Tel: (01923) 664258.

Building Research
Establishment, *The School
Toolkit*, A guide for reducing
costs and environmental
impacts, 1996, is available on
computer disc from the
BREEAM Office,
Tel: 01923 664462
Fax: 01923 664103

**Organisations promoting
energy conservation in
schools**
BRECSU - Department of the
Environment sponsored advice
on best practice and design
(address above).

EST - manages energy
conservation schemes and
grants,
Energy Saving Trust,
11-12 Buckingham Gate,
London, SW1E 6LB.
Tel: 0171 931 8401
Fax: 0171 931 85488

CREATE - national coordinating
body for energy education,
The Centre for Research,
Education and Training in
Energy, Kenley House,
25 Bridgeman Terrace,
Wigan, WN1 1TD.
Tel: 01942 322271.

Energy management

The management of a building can enhance or nullify the design effort expended to achieve efficiency and low fuel consumption. As these guidelines are intended to aid energy conservation in existing buildings as well as in new, a short summary of good management practice is appropriate. Staff and pupils should be made aware of the issues and encouraged to play their part in energy management.

Checklist of energy management measures

1 In the heating season, do not cool overheated rooms by opening windows or using extractor fans. Adjust the heating system instead, and where possible set thermostats to give the recommended room temperatures. If additional ventilation is still required, open windows the minimum amount or use fans for the minimum period. Excess ventilation causes over-cooling and an increase in the heating requirement.

2 Economise on the use of hot water, subject of course to the need for cleanliness and hygiene. The use of spray taps and/or a decentralized system helps to minimise energy waste. Caretaking and purchasing staff should be given information on cold water cleaning compounds. These can eliminate the need for hot water for cleaning during periods out of normal school hours.

3 Encourage staff and pupils to wear clothes that are suitable for the required temperatures.

4 If separate zones of a building can be heated independently, allocate rooms for both daytime and use out of school hours so that the plant is used economically, and heat and light are not supplied to unused areas.

5 Start heating plant no earlier than is necessary to achieve normal working temperatures by the beginning of the occupied period. The plant can also be turned off some time before the end of occupation. Optimum stop/start controls can achieve this. If a building energy management system is installed a member of staff should be trained to use it and be responsible for its operation.

6 External doors should be kept closed as much as possible in cold weather and all windows closed overnight. Blinds or curtains drawn at dusk will help conserve heat overnight.

7 Equipment with high electrical power consumption should not be used at times during the winter months when the total electrical load from other sources is likely to be near the 'Maximum Demand' limit. The maximum demand meter measures the amount of electricity being used at any instant. The highest reading in any month or quarter (depending on the tariff) is often used to calculate the standing charge. The increase in standing charge caused by exceeding the limit can increase the cost of the electricity for the winter quarter by as much as three times.

Energy (carbon dioxide) rating calculation sheet

Floor area _____ square metres excluding kitchens and swimming pools

Factors for use with Figure 3 in lighting calculation

Average room depth _____ metres

Window : wall ratio _____ percentage glazing on internal elevation of external wall

Occupancy _____ persons

Density of occupancy _____ square metres of gross floor area per person

Design temperature   Internal _____ °C

           External _____ °C   Local 20-year degree day average _____

           Temperature difference _____ °C

Model year factors page 28   W _____   School days in heating season _____   DR _____ R_p _____ D_l _____

Losses		Area	U-value	Watts/m^2
Opaque area page 33(a)	Walls			
	Roof			
	Floor			
Windows	North			
	South			
	East			
	West			
	Rooflights			

Ventilation rate _____ m^3/hour/person   Ventilation loss page 33(b) _____ Watts/m^2

Convert to kWh/m^2: (divide by 1000 and multiply by corrected equilvalent hours of operation _____)   **kWh/m^2**

Gains

Incidental	Installed load (W/m^2)	Hours of operation	kWh/m^2
Miscellaneous power page 33(c)			
Lighting from Figure 3 page 33(d)			

	Metabolic rate (W/person)	Hours of occupancy	
Occupancy page 33(e)			

Factors for solar gain calculation page 31

Transmission of glazing T _____   Utility factor f _____   Shadow factor T_s _____

Solar gain factor

Solar gain pages 31 and 33(f)	Area	Average solar radiation	Solar gain	kWh/m^2
North				
South				
East				
West				
Rooflights				
Sum of solar gains				

Total gains				**kWh/m^2**

Heating requirement: losses – gains				**kWh/m^2**
Delivered fuel equivalent:	(divide by heating system efficiency	_____)		**kWh/m^2**
Carbon dioxide equivalent:	(multiply by carbon dioxide conversion factor	_____)		**KgCO$_2$/m^2 (i)**

Other uses	Installed Load (W/m^2)	Hours of operation	kWh/m^2
Domestic hot water			
Delivered fuel equivalent:	(divide by hot water system efficiency _____)		
Carbon dioxide equivalent:	(multiply by carbon dioxide conversion factor _____)		**KgCO$_2$/m^2 (ii)**

Electrical energy	Installed Load (W/m^2)	Hours of operation	kWh/m^2
Lighting (Figure 3)			
Miscellaneous power			
Heating circulators			
Total electric			**kWh/m^2**
Carbon dioxide equivalent:	(multiply by carbon dioxide conversion factor _____)		**KgCO$_2$/m^2 (iii)**

Total Annual Carbon Dioxide Production Value
(heating + hot water + electrical) (i + ii + iii) _____   **Kg carbon dioxide per square metre of gross floor area**

Section F: Energy (carbon dioxide) rating

Energy (carbon dioxide) rating spreadsheet formula sheet

	A	B	C	D	E	F	G	H	I
1	Floor area exc. kitchens & swimming pools				square metres.				
2									
3	Factors for use with Figure 3								
4	Average room depth				metres				
5	Window: wall ratio				percentage glazing on internal elevation of external wall				
6									
7	Occupancy				persons				
8	Density of occupation		=C1/C7		square metres of gross floor area per person				
9	Model year factors page 28	W	0.8				Days in school heating season	144	
10		Rp	0.7	DI	0.96		DR	=H9/176	
11									
12	Design temperature	Internal			degrees Centigrade				
13		External			degrees Centigrade				
14		Temperature difference		=D12-D13	degrees Centigrade		Local 20-year degree day average		
15									
16									
17	Losses		Area	U-value	Watts/m2				
18	Opaque areas (page 33(a))	Walls			=D18 x C18 x $D$14/$C$1				
19		Roof			=D19 x C19 x $D$14/$C$1				
20		Floor			=D20 x C20 x $D$14/$C$1				
21	Windows	North			=D21 x C21 x $D$14/$C$1				
22		South			=D22 x C22 x $D$14/$C$1				
23		East			=D23 x C23 x $D$14/$C$1				
24		West			=D24 x C24 x $D$14/$C$1				
25		Rooflights			=D25 x C25 x $D$14/$C$1				
26									
27	Ventilation rate	=D27/0.2778	m3/person/hour		litres/second/person	Vent loss(page 33(b))	=(B27 x 0.33 x D14/C8)	Watts/m2	
28									
29	Total losses: (fabric + ventilation losses)				=SUM(E18:E25)+G27			Watts/m2	
30									
31	Convert to kWh/m2: (divide by 1000)								
32	and multiply by corrected equivalent hours of operation				=24 x H14 x1.3 x C9 x H10 x C10 x E10/D14)		=E29 x (E32/1000)	kWh/m2	
33									
34									
35	Gains								
36	Incidental								
37			Installed Load(W/m2)			Hours of operation			
38	Miscellaneous power page 33(c)		5			1020	=D38 x F38/1000	kWh/m2	
39	Lighting page 33(d)						=0.8 x F63	kWh/m2	
40			Metabolic rate						
41			(W/person)			Hours of occupancy			
42	Occupancy page 33(e)		70			680	=(D42 x F42 x $C$7)/($C$1 x 1000)	kWh/m2	
43									
44	Factors for solar gain calculation page 31								
45	Transmission of glazing T	0.76	Utility factor f	0.65	Shadow factor TS	0.8			
46	Solar gain factor	=100*D45*F45*B45*C9*H10*C10*E10/C1							
47									
48	Solar gains pages 31 and 33(f)			Area	Average Solar radiation on vertical surface		Solar gains	kWh/m2	
49		North					=D49*$B$46*E49		
50		South					=D50*$B$46*E50		
51		East					=D51*$B$46*E51		
52		West					=D52*$B$46*E52		
53		Rooflights					=D53*$B$46*E53		
54		Sum of solar gains					=SUM(G49+G50+G51+G52+G53)		
55	Total gains						=G38+G39+G42+G54	kWh/m2	
56									
57	Heating Requirement: Losses - gains						=G32-G55		
58	Delivered fuel equivalent: (divide by heating system efficiency)					)	=G57/E58	kWh/m2	
59	Carbon dioxide equivalent: (multiply by carbon dioxide conversion factor)					)	=G58 x E59	KgCO2/m2 (i)	
60									
61	Other uses				Installed load (W/m2)		Hours of operation		
62	Domestic hot water		2			1500	=D62 x F62/1000	kWh/m2	
63	Delivered fuel equivalent (divide by hot water system efficiency)					)	=G62/E63	kWh/m2	
64	Carbon dioxide equivalent: (multiply by carbon dioxide conversion factor)					)	=G63 x E64	KgCO2/m2 (ii)	
65									
66	Electrical energy		Installed load (W/m2)		Hours of operation	kWh/m2			
67	Lighting (Figure 3)					8.8			
68	Miscellaneous power		5		1500	=C68 x E68/1000			
69	Heating circulators		2		1200	=C69 x E69/1000			
70	Total electric						=F67+F68+F69	kWh/m2	
71	Carbon dioxide equivalent: (multiply by carbon dioxide conversion factor)					)	=G70 x E71	KgCO2/m2 (iii)	
72									
73	Total Annual Carbon Dioxide Production Value								
74	(heating + hot water + electrical)	(i+ii+iii)			=G59+G64+G71	Kg carbon dioxide per square metre of gross floor area			

The School Premises Regulations summary sheet

Acoustics

Each room or other space in a school building shall have the acoustic conditions and the insulation against disturbance by noise appropriate to its normal use.

Lighting

(1) Each room or other space in a school building -

    (a) shall have lighting appropriate to its normal use; and

    (b) shall satisfy the requirements of paragraphs (2) to (4).

(2) Subject to paragraph (3), the maintained illuminance of teaching accommodation shall be not less than 300 lux on the working plane.

(3) In teaching accommodation where visually demanding tasks are carried out, provision shall be made for a maintained illuminance of not less than 500 lux on the working plane.

(4) The glare Index shall be limited to no more than 19.

Heating

(1) Each room or other space in a school building shall have such system of heating, if any, as is appropriate to its normal use.

(2) Any such heating system shall be capable of maintaining in the areas set out in column (1) of the Table below the air temperature set opposite thereto, in column (2) of that Table, at a height of 0.5m above floor level when the external air temperature is -1°C:

(1) Area	(2) Temperature
Areas where there is the normal level of physical activity associated with teaching, private study or examinations	18°C.
Areas where there is a lower than normal level of physical activity because of sickness or physical disability including sick rooms and isolation rooms but not other sleeping accommodation	21°C.
Areas where there is a higher than normal level of physical activity (for example arising out of physical education) and washrooms, sleeping accommodation and circulation spaces.	15°C.

(3) Each room or other space which has a heating system shall, if the temperature during any period during which it is occupied would otherwise be below that appropriate to its normal use, be heated to a temperature which is so appropriate.

(4) In a special school, nursery school or teaching accommodation used by a nursery class in a school the surface temperature of any radiator, including exposed pipework, which is in a position where it may be touched by a pupil shall not exceed 43°C.

Ventilation

(1) All occupied areas in a school building shall have controllable ventilation at a minimum rate of 3 litres of fresh air per second for each of the maximum number of persons the area will accommodate.

(2) All teaching accommodation, medical examination or treatment rooms, sick rooms, isolation rooms, sleeping and living accommodation shall also be capable of being ventilated at a minimum rate of 8 litres of fresh air per second for each of the usual number of people in those areas when such areas are occupied.

(3) All washrooms shall also be capable of being ventilated at a rate of at least six air changes an hour.

(4) Adequate measures shall be taken to prevent condensation in, and remove noxious fumes from, every kitchen and other room in which there may be steam or fumes.

Water supplies

(1) A school shall have a wholesome supply of water for domestic purposes including a supply of drinking water.

(2) Water closets and urinals shall have an adequate supply of cold water and washbasins, sinks, baths and showers shall have an adequate supply of hot and cold water.

(3) The temperature of hot water supplies to baths and showers shall not exceed 43°C.

Drainage

(1) A school shall be provided with an adequate drainage system for hygienic purposes and the general disposal of waste water and surface water.

Recommended constructional standards summary sheet

Acoustics

Values for maximum permissible background noise level and minimum sound insulation between rooms are given in Tables 1a and 1b and values for reverberation times are given in Table 2 in Section A.

Lighting

Priority should be given to daylight as the main source of light in working areas, except in special circumstances. Wherever possible a daylit space should have an average daylight factor of 4–5%.

The uniformity ratio (minimum/average maintained illuminance) of the electric lighting in teaching areas should be not less than 0.8 over the task area.

Teaching spaces should have views out except in special circumstances. A minimum glazed area of 20% of the internal elevation of the exterior wall is recommended to provide adequate views out.

A maintained illuminance at floor level in the range 80 - 120 lux is recommended for stairs and corridors.

Entrance halls, lobbies and waiting rooms require a higher illuminance in the range 175 - 250 lux on the appropriate plane.

The type of luminaires should be chosen to give an average initial circuit luminous efficacy of 65 lumens/circuit watt for the fixed lighting equipment within the building, excluding track-mounted luminaires and emergency lighting.

Heating

The heating system should be capable of maintaining the minimum air temperatures quoted in the School Premises Regulations. The heating system should be provided with frost protection.

During the summer, when the heating system is not in operation, the recommended design temperature for all spaces should be $23^{\circ}C$ with a swing of not more than +/- $4^{\circ}C$. It is undesirable for peak air temperatures to exceed $28^{\circ}C$ during normal working hours but a higher temperature on 10 days during the summer term is considered a reasonable predictive risk.

The air supply to and discharge of products of combustion from heat producing appliances and the protection of the building from the appliances and their flue pipes and chimneys should comply with Building Regulations, Part J, 1990.

Thermal performance

The recommended maximum values of average thermal transmittance coefficients (calculated using the 'Proportional Area Method' used in the Building Regulations, Part L, 1994) are:

	$W/m^{2o}C$
• Walls	0.4
• Roof	0.3
• Roof with a loft space	0.25
• Floor	0.4
• Doors, windows and rooflights	2.8

Vertical glazed areas (including clerestory or monitor lights) should not normally exceed an average of 40% of the internal elevation of the external wall. However, where a passive solar or daylight design strategy has been adopted the percentage glazing may well exceed 40%. Also in areas prone to breakages due to vandalism the replacement cost may justify the use of single glazing instead of double glazing. In these cases the insulation of the rest of the building fabric should be increased to compensate for the increased heat loss through the glazing.

Horizontal or near horizontal glazing should not normally exceed 20% of the roof area.

Ventilation

The heating system should be capable of maintaining the required room air temperatures with the minimum average background ventilation of 3 litres per second of fresh air per person.

Spaces where noxious fumes or dust are generated may need additional ventilation. Laboratories may require the use of fume cupboards, which should be designed in accordance with DfEE Design Note 29. Design technology areas may require local exhaust ventilation.

All washrooms in which at least 6 air changes per hour cannot be achieved on average by natural means should be mechanically ventilated and the air expelled from the building.

Hot and cold water

Cold water storage capacity in day schools should not exceed 25 litres per occupant.

All water fittings should be of a type approved by the WRC (Water Research Centre), and all installations should comply with the Water Supplies Byelaws (to be replaced by the Water Regulations).

Where a temperature regime is used to reduce the risk of *legionellosis*, hot water storage temperatures should not be lower than $60^{\circ}C$. However for occupant safety, to reduce the risk of scalding, The School Premises Regulations require that the temperature at point of use should not be above $43^{\circ}C$ for baths and showers and where occupants are severely disabled. This may be achieved by thermostatic mixing at the point of use. It is also recommended that hot water supplies to washbasins in nursery and primary schools are limited to $43^{\circ}C$.

Particular attention should be given to the provision of facilities to ensure the effective maintenance of systems.

Unvented hot water storage systems should comply with Building Regulations, Part G3, 1992.

Energy (carbon dioxide) rating

In the design of a new building the calculated Annual CO_2 Production Value should be below the top of band D shown in Figure 1 or 2 (on page 27), when the environmental standards in Sections B and C have been achieved.

Printed in the UK by The Stationery Office Limited
10/97 324353 19585 (CRC supplied)